T0181368

ADVANCED TOPICS
IN SCIENCE AND TECHNOLOGY IN CHINA

ADVANCED TOPICS
IN SCIENCE AND TECHNOLOGY IN CHINA

Zhejiang University is one of the leading universities in China. In Advanced Topics in Science and Technology in China, Zhejiang University Press and Springer jointly publish monographs by Chinese scholars and professors, as well as invited authors and editors from abroad who are outstanding experts and scholars in their fields. This series will be of interest to researchers, lecturers, and graduate students alike.

Advanced Topics in Science and Technology in China aims to present the latest and most cutting-edge theories, techniques, and methodologies in various research areas in China. It covers all disciplines in the fields of natural science and technology, including but not limited to, computer science, materials science, life sciences, engineering, environmental sciences, mathematics, and physics.

For further volumes:
http://www.springer.com/series/7887

Zhaohui Wu • Gang Pan

SmartShadow: Models and Methods for Pervasive Computing

Zhaohui Wu
Gang Pan
Department of Computer Science
Zhejiang University
Hangzhou, China, People's Republic

ISSN 1995-6819   ISSN 1995-6827 (electronic)
ISBN 978-3-642-42964-4   ISBN 978-3-642-36382-5 (eBook)
DOI 10.1007/978-3-642-36382-5
Springer Heidelberg New York Dordrecht London

Jointly published with Zhejiang University Press, Hangzhou
ISBN: 978-7-308-09799-4 Zhejiang University Press, Hangzhou

Preface

Pervasive computing is becoming an emerging paradigm of next-generation computing. It seeks to transform computer-centric computing to human-centered computing. Its goal is to build a personal living environment where digital services can be provided seamlessly at the right time at the right place in the right way. Pervasive computing is an innovation of information and computing technology, which leads to revolution in the relationship between the physical environment of human life and the cyberspace. It will greatly change our future way of life.

This book compiles some recent work from the Pervasive Computing Group of the CCNT (advanCed Computing aNd sysTem) laboratory at Zhejiang University, China. Pervasive computing, as a new computing model, spans a number of research areas with unprecedented complexity and diversity. This book describes a new model for pervasive computing, called *SmartShadow*, and its methods. A good model is not only essential to abstractly model "user-oriented" environments which is the core philosophy of pervasive computing, but which is also important in design, analysis, implementation, deployment, assessment of pervasive computing systems to support such systems with a wide range of theoretical guidance for the scalability, maintainability, adaptability, ease of use, and standardization at the model-level. The organization of the book is as follows. Chapter 1 gives an overview of the SmartShadow. It consists of a user model which represents information about of a user's personality (called *PersonalityShadow*) and a space model which represents a virtual smart space of services following a user (called *ServiceShadow*). Chapter 2 describes how a user task in the SmartShadow can migrate continuously and seamlessly between different physical spaces when users move from one to another. Context-awareness is strongly related to how smart a system is, which is presented in Chap. 3. We propose a three-layer context model in the SmartShadow to handle large-scale contextual data. In Chap. 4, we describe a new file management scheme to link files with contextual data in SmartShadow, so that we can have a human-oriented view of file dynamics. Chapter 5 builds a software infrastructure with semantics and high adaptation to support the SmartShadow. Chapter 6 presents a smart car prototype to demonstrate an application of the SmartShadow.

This book would not have been possible without many contributors whose names did not make it to the cover. We would like to give our special thanks to Mr. Li Zhang, Mr. Yuqiong Xu, Dr. Qing Wu, Dr. Jie Sun, Dr. Yanfei Liu, Dr. Shijian Li, Mrs. Tong Li, and Mr. Qunjie Qiu, who have been affiliated to the CCNT (advanCed Computing aNd sysTem) laboratory of Zhejiang University. For a long time already, it has been our pleasure to do research with them in pervasive computing. They have devoted their energy and enthusiasm to this area and relevant research projects.

The work in this book was mainly supported by the National Science Fund for Distinguished Young Scholars (No. 60525202), the Natural Science Foundation of China (No. 61070067, No. 60533040), the National Key Basic Research Program of China (No. 2013CB329504), the National 863 High-Tech Program (No. 2009AA011900, No. 2008AA01Z132, No. 2006AA01Z198), the Program for New Century Excellent Talents in University (NCET-04-0545), Zhejiang Provincial Natural Science Foundation (No. RC01058, No. Y1090690), and Qianjiang Talent Program of Zhejiang (2011R10078).

Hangzhou, China   Zhaohui Wu
October 2012   Gang Pan

Contents

Chapter 1
SmartShadow Model

Abstract Pervasive computing has become an emerging paradigm of next-generation computing. This chapter attempts to model pervasive computing as a user-centric model *SmartShadow*, which contains a model of users and a model of computing environments. In the user model, we model user-related temporal information in three parts, raw data, activity/behavior, and intention. The user model is used to describe and infer users' needs and tasks. The environment model considers all the computing entities in a pervasive computing enviroment as pervasive services. With both models, the pervasive computing environment of a user can be modeled as a dynamic virtual user space, which follows him/her with services anytime anywhere, just like his/her shadow in the physical world.

1.1 Introduction

Pervasive computing [1] seeks to transform computer-centric computing to human-centered computing. Its goal is to build a personal computing environment that makes use of computing and communication resources in surroundings. Digital services can provide human-centered services seamlessly at the right time at the right place in the right way. Pervasive computing is an innovation of information society development, which leads to revolutionary change in the relationship between the physical environment of human life and the information environment provided by computers. Pervasive computing will greatly change our future way of life.

Pervasive computing, as a new computing model, spans a number of research areas with unprecedented complexity and diversity. Though, currently, various technologies have been researched, little has been addressed on the pervasive computing model. A good model is not only essential to abstractly model "user-oriented" environments which is the core philosophy of pervasive computing, but which is also important in design, analysis, implementation, deployment, and assessment

Z. Wu and G. Pan, *SmartShadow: Models and Methods for Pervasive Computing*, Advanced Topics in Science and Technology in China, DOI 10.1007/978-3-642-36382-5_1, © Zhejiang University Press, Hangzhou and Springer-Verlag Berlin Heidelberg 2013

of pervasive computing systems to support such systems with a wide range of theoretical guidance for the scalability, maintainability, adaptability, ease of use, and standardization at the model level [2].

For complexity characteristics of pervasive computing patterns, early researchers proposed a number of hierarchical models. Dima et al. proposed a hierarchical conceptual model for pervasive computing. With reference to the Open Systems Interconnection Model (OSI model) for computer networks, they model pervasive computing with a bottom-up model divided into five parts: the environmental layer, physical layer, resource layer, abstraction layer, and intention layer [3]. Muhlhauser et al. proposed a three-tier model [4] for pervasive computing, based on granularity and integration degree. Pervasive computing concepts are divided into three levels: the base components level, integration level. and universal-world level, in which the integration level is a software system that supports scalability and adaptability. Henricksen et al. divide pervasive computing into four elements: devices, users, software components, and user interfaces, in which software components and devices can dynamically form a complete application with user interface to interact with users [5]. Xu et al. analyzed related scientific problems and view pervasive environments as a duality of physical space and cyber space [6]. Dual relations between cyber space and physical space are established using human–computer interaction (HCI). Such models are based more on the perspective of system hierarchies which only describe coarse-grained computing entities and lack support for describing the interactive and dynamic nature of pervasive computing environments.

Recently, researchers have carried out several studies on more issues relating to a pervasive computing system, such as functional verification, interoperability, equipment, architecture at the model and theoretical level. Ranganathan et al. proposed a pervasive computing model based on environment (ambient) calculus and logic, in which any description of the environment can be formally verified for its function and role. This model is adopted in a prototype application on the Gaia system [7]. Blackstock et al. designed a general model called UCM for assessment and analysis on interoperation in pervasive computing environments, and this model is based on their analysis of existing systems and development experience and provides some high-level abstraction for pervasive computing systems to characterize interoperability of devices and software components. Scott de Deugd et al. put forward Service-Oriented Device Architecture (SODA) [8], by which devices can be used as a service to service-oriented software architecture, which enhances system scalability and flexibility. Costa et al. are dedicated to design a common software infrastructure for pervasive computing space [9]. They have produced ten keys and seven challenges across every aspect of the life of a pervasive computing system.

The works above reflect some new research trends regarding the models and architectures of pervasive computing research, so as to abstract the computing resources over a wide range into a group of basic entities, to focus on interactions between cyber space and physical space, and to adopt service-oriented views of system constructions. However, rarely is research taking place on pervasive computing to model computing entities and the environment as a whole.

This chapter introduces a ubiquitous computing model called *SmartShadow*. Some part of the work has been published as [10, 39]. The model is based on the modeling of users and smart environments. In this model, the context of the environment and the intentions of users can be dynamically mapped into a collaboration of pervasive services as a user-centered virtual personal space. This model can achieve an environment-and-user-aware adaptive pervasive service. Established in our model, dynamic user-service mapping makes pervasive services act as a shadow following the user moving across spaces, and automatically adapts to the "light source" (environment context and services).

1.2 SmartShadow: An Overview

Differing from previous pervasive computing models, SmartShadow contains a user model that represents information about a user's personality and a space model that represents a virtual smart space of services following a user and serving him in different environments. Information for user personality (called *PersonalityShadow*) can be sensed, recorded, and learned, which implies the user's personal lifestyle, behavior, and thinking; a virtual smart space (called *ServiceShadow*) is a composition of environment computing resources to work for users' intentions. PersonalityShadow and ServiceShadow together described the interaction between users and environments.

In order to build a sophisticated model to appropriately explain how user cognitions, activities, and desires are generated under certain environments and how environments satisfy such desires, we have deeply studied internal relationships between the user and the environment. We expect our model will significantly improve pervasive computing systems in understanding and adapting to users and environments. Our goal falls into twofolds: one is to learn everyday life of users from gathering sufficient data to describe their life, the other is to learn how to satisfy user desires with computing resources in pervasive computing environments.

1.2.1 PersonalityShadow: Model of People's Life

PersonalityShadow is actually about relations between context and people's life. Using context as an input to characterize the environment and to reason about user desires is one of the major characteristics of ubiquitous computing. This research is known as context-aware computing. Context-aware computing is a computing paradigm in which applications can sense, react, and adapt to their environment. In a context-aware system, the most important information is the state of the environment, the devices, and the users, which we call context. Context is any information that can be used to characterize the situation of an entity.

Current context-aware computing systems with their models are not sufficient to model all factors in people's life, because there are plenty of factors that are hard to sense and predict, such as the psychological state of a person or activities involving many people. Such features as activities and physical-psychology status reflect the higher-level lifestyle of people, which makes the sensed context meaningful and actually connects user requirements and computing applications. Such higher-level information is more useful and important than sensed context but there exist gaps between lower-level information and higher-level information that make models of pervasive computing incomplete.

We propose the PersonalityShadow that covers almost all aspects of a person's life. The PersonalityShadow is divided into three stages: low-level personal information, mid-level personal information, and high-level personal information according to semantic levels and relative convenience. The low-level personal status can be directly sensed using sensors, the mid-level needs pattern recognition or inference, and the high-level hides the internal user's mind. We believe context states at the lower level can influence context at the higher level, and the higher level is more decisive regarding a user's intentions and requirements. In our work, we enumerate a great number of characteristics of user's life and classify them into the three levels accordingly. We also provide intelligence to manage such information and to infer higher-level status. The PersonalityShadow literally follows its owner moving around across different environments to make computing environments know his lifestyle.

1.2.2 ServiceShadow: User-Centered Virtual Space

Pervasive computing environments are full of software, devices, sensors, actuators, and web services that can be used as computing resources. By reasoning context information and user personality, an environment can obtain a user's intention. Then the environment can integrate suitable services to collaborate with the intention to form a user-centric virtual space called ServiceShadow or SmartShadow Space.

We propose a model of the environment, in which the environmental context is characterized. Any computing resources of software and hardware are viewed as services. A ServiceShadow is a group of composite services to serve user intentions as shown in Fig. 1.1. When a user moves, the ServiceShadow follows him to another place, migrates service status to new local services, and keeps uninterrupted execution; and if the environment context affects service quality, the ServiceShadow adapts itself accordingly to behavior and resources to achieve seamless user experience. We also proposed approaches to handle service integration for user intention and adaptation in different conditions to keep the ServiceShadow seamlessly serving with satisfactory quality.

A comparison of ServiceShadow with other smart spaces is shown in Table 1.1. ServiceShadow is a user-centric space, which follows the mobile user and adapts to environment dynamics.

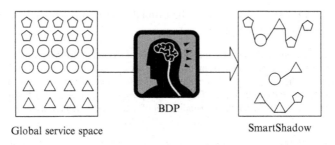

Fig. 1.1 Mapping to a virtual service

Table 1.1 Comparison between ServiceShadow and smart space

	Mobility	Dynamics	Abstractness	User-centric organization
Smart Spaces	Static	Weak	Physical	No
ServiceShadow	Mobile (like a shadow)	Strong	Virtual	Yes

1.3   Semantics in SmartShadow

For a uniform description of various users and spaces, a semantic model for
SmartShadow is essential to specify characteristics of human personality, computing resources, environment, and relative management mechanisms to monitor
environment context, to infer user status and desires or to integrate/coordinate
behavior and resources of computing services.

1.3.1   Basic Concepts

The concept "Semantics" is a study about meanings and relationships between
different meanings. This concept is originally about word and form changing in
the development of languages. But today it contains many new ideas from the past
to the technology. "In linguistics, it is the study of interpretation of signs or symbols
as used by agents or communities within particular circumstances and contexts.
Within this view, sounds, facial expressions, body language, proxemics has semantic
(meaningful) content, and each has several branches of study. In written language,
such things as paragraph structure and punctuation have semantic content; in other
forms of language, there is other semantic content" [12].

   To make computing systems understand the meaning of the world, the Semantic
Web is proposed. The Semantic Web [13] is an evolving extension of the World
Wide Web in which web resources are annotated, identified, and interlinked in
a meaningful way, thus permitting software agents to find, share, and integrate

information more easily and readily. The official website of W3C's Semantic Web gives a more definitive description:

> The Semantic Web is about two things. It is about common formats for integration and combination of data drawn from diverse sources, where the original Web mainly concentrated on the interchange of documents. It is also about language for recording how the data relates to real world objects. That allows a person, or a machine, to start off in one database, and then move through an unending set of databases which are connected not by wires but by being about the same thing.

The Semantic Web draws on the standardization effort of a formal representation framework for describing the semantics of web resources. The semantic theory underlying this formal representation framework provides a formal account of "meaning" in which the logical relationship of web resources, which can be a webpage, a database record, a program, a web service, and so forth, can be explicitly described and specified without loss of the original meaning. Functionally speaking, it would enable us to aggregate and recombine the right data we want seamlessly and instantly; for example, automatic scheduling of a meeting across the calendars of different people, arranging travels based on the profiles of both providers and requestors, facilitating integrative knowledge discovery from an unbound set of data repositories, etc.

As the crucial thing for realizing the vision is a well-defined resource description model and web languages for sharing meanings, the standard organizations, like the Internet Engineering Task Force and the World Wide Web Consortium (W3C), have devoted and directed major efforts at specifying, developing, and deploying the semantic web languages.

In 1999, the W3C released the first semantic web standard, the Resource Description Framework (RDF) specification, as a W3C recommendation. RDF provides a simple but powerful triple-based representation language for describing web resources and the relationship among them. The simplicity consists in the triple statement model, which actually cannot be any simpler for describing something in the world. This simplicity guarantees the extensibility and adaptability for future development.

The RDF Schema [14], as a basic vocabulary language, became a recommendation in February 2004. RDFS takes the basic RDF specification and extends it to support the expression of structured vocabularies such as classes and properties. It provides the basic constructs to develop ontology but lacks the necessary expressiveness for many advanced applications.

For those who require greater expressiveness in their object and relation descriptions, OWL (the Web Ontology Language) [15] is the choice. OWL has more advanced facilities and representing constructs such as those for describing property restrictions, concept cardinality, making it a fully-fledged knowledge representation language capable of describing knowledge from simple metadata such as tags to complex conceptual models such as a biological ontology.

As the semantic languages have gained ground and mature, commercial RDF/OWL reasoners and stores have also been ready at customers' disposal, the need arises for reliable and standardized access to the RDF data they hold. The SPARQL language [16], which became a W3C recommendation in 2007, was designed to meet this requirement. SPARQL can be viewed as the standardized ontology query language for retrieving and querying the RDF repository.

Furthermore, other significant progress includes the GRDDL (Gleaning Resource Descriptions from Dialects of Languages) [17], which provides a means to extract RDF from XML and XHTML documents using transformations expressed in XSLT (Extensible Stylesheet Language), and the Rule Interchange Format, an attempt to support and interoperate across a variety of rule-based formats, by which more advanced rule-based reasoning capability can be enabled.

Most recently, more advanced efforts have been made on top of these standards and technologies. For example, the suggested Named Graph [18] allows users to attach contextual information such as digital signature, trust policies, time stamps, provenance information, etc., onto a group of RDF assertions. The extension of RDF to Named Graphs provides a formally defined framework to be a foundation for the Semantic Web trust layer.

Along with the busy production line of the standardization effort are the phenomenal endeavors in industry-level tool development and commercialization, such as Jena.

1.3.2   Models and Systems in Pervasive Computing

Semantic models have been widely used to describe context information in pervasive computing. Context is any information that can be used to characterize the status of an entity [19]. An entity may be a person, a place, or an object that is considered relevant to the interaction between a user and an application, including the user and application themselves. Commonly used contexts consist of location, identity, time, temperature, and activity. We consider that the involved objects in environments are all contexts. Context awareness is the ability to sense and use different contexts. Any application that takes advantage of context is a context-aware application. Context-aware computing is the ability of computing devices to detect, interpret, and respond to changes in environment and system. The semantic information of contexts is essential for dealing with the complex tasks in ubiquitous computing environments. However, representing sharing and reasoning of the contexts is very difficult. In smart spaces, context is hard to represent and use due to its complexity. It requires an approach with strong expression and easy sharing capabilities and many research works have investigated these issues.

CoBrA (Context Broker Architecture) proposes a semantic broker approach that explores the use of semantic web languages in building an architecture for supporting context-aware systems [19]. CoBrA is an agent-based system that supports smart spaces (e.g., offices, smart homes, and cars) with context brokers. Context brokers are intelligent agents that share a common model of context semantics. CoBrA uses the Web Ontology Language OWL, a W3C Semantic Web standard, to define ontologies of context (people, agents, devices, events, time, space, etc.) with strong expressive power to support context reasoning and high-level knowledge sharing.

ASC Model (Aspect-Scale-Context Information) is proposed by Thomas Strang [20]. ASC defines the semantics of core concepts of the computing environment with ontology, which guarantees sharing and reuse of context knowledge. In the ASC model, an aspect is used to manage several scales and a scale accumulates several context informations. Each scale defines a valid range of context information. In order to implement the ASC model, CoOL (Context Ontology Language) is proposed. This language can be divided into two parts, CoOL core and CoOL sets. CoOL core maps model to commonly used ontology languages, such as OWL, DAML+OIL, and F-LOGIC to predigest development of knowledge. CoOL sets include the framework, protocols, and standards to make CoOL core feasible in any systems such as a web service.

CONON provides common concepts of context-awareness and enables users to add a new concept into the model [21]. There are two types of concepts in CONON: upper ontology and domain-specific ontologies. Upper ontology defines common characteristics of location, users, and computing entities that form the framework of the model and index of concept information. Domain-specific ontologies define concepts in different application domains in which applications and services can be divided into different subdomains such as home applications or office applications. Concepts in a different domain share a common model but are distinct in characteristics. The CONON model defines 14 sets of core entities. Each entity represents a physical or conceptual object such as users, behavior, computing entities, and locations.

SOUPA ontology includes two parts: SOUPA core, which defines common onlotogy in a pervasive computing domain, SOUPA extensions, which define specific application domains [22]. SOUPA core includes modularized definitions about users, smart agents, time, space, events, user profiles, behavior, privacy, and security policy and forms nine distinct ontology documents. SOUPA extensions define concepts in a specific application domain, currently supporting context-aware applications and P2P data management of conference, schedules, documents, images, and locations.

Nexus Project aims to establish a global platform to manage context semantics. It provides a uniform standard for modeling context by enabling any context model to join in the platform. This standard is a global object-oriented ontology and defines context sharing between application and data providers. The keystone of the project is to research how to manage local models in a global view [23].

1.3.3 Semantic Issues in SmartShadow

Built on top of techniques such as Semantic Web, SmartShadow is dedicated to modern scientific research on user-awareness and smart space management, which faces several challenges calling for more innovative approaches. Below, we identify a set of basic issues concerned with SmartShadow.

1.3.3.1 Knowledge Representation for SmartShadow

In people's life and environment, there is a significantly huge amount of personal information, including context, physical–psychological status, behavior, activities, and desires. Also, heterogeneous computing resources, including sensors, actuators, software components, devices, web services, etc. The diversity and heterogeneous nature of SmartShadow calls for a more advanced knowledge model to describe these contents formally, explicitly, with flexibility and scalability, so as to enable more intelligent mechanisms for context management, event and intention inference, automated service discovery, matching, integration and resource coordination. The ontology language and related techniques can play an important role in alleviating the problem and facilitating information exchange. Formal rules are useful for specifying personality status, coordination policy, security settings, transaction configurations, trust dependencies, etc.

1.3.3.2 Semantic-Based Personality Inference

Inference of user personality is essential in SmartShadow to capture user requirements. The PersonalityShadow model aims to integrate many rich-semantic descriptions of people's personalities to recommend appropriate entities or arrange services for users whose requirements need to be inferred from formal semantic descriptions about his/her personality. We need semantic-based and formal inference mechanisms.

1.3.3.3 Semantic Service Composition and Resource Coordination

ServiceShadow constitutes various computing resources that are viewed as services, so service descriptions, discovery, registration, and composition are common requirements of all smart spaces. But heterogeneous systems may have different implementations, although they are used for identical missions. To orchestrate such a ServiceShadow, it is crucial to provide unified ways to represent the process semantics and bridge the discrepancies and mismatches among different service models. We need to adopt semantically enriched service descriptions and manage to pursue more advanced service interaction and collaboration.

1.3.3.4 Semantics for Trust and Security

One defining characteristic of a smart space is the need for trust and security. In such an open environment with multiple users and services involved, trust management and related security issues such as authentication, encryption, and privacy are even more intrusive and tricky. SmartShadow requires all of these issues to be handled with as minimal as possible human intervention. We need to solve a relevant problem, namely, how to represent and describe the trust dependencies and security policies, so that the semantics of access control can be uniformly communicated with consistent interpretation.

1.4 Modeling Human Personalities

Inspired by the recent progress in cognitive science [24], we propose a personality model that divides factors of user life into three stages, namely, low-level personal information, mid-level personal information, and high-level personal information. Each stage plays a unique role in predicting user status and needs. Recalling the process to form one's consciousness, firstly, one must record a short-time memory about something, such as a patient who caught a cold feels many bad effects such as headache, fever, cough, etc. After many days, the patient will forget the actual bodily feelings, only to remember such bad feelings are the symptoms of a cold. He can further conclude how to treat a cold as a personal belief. This procedure illustrates an evolution from low-level information to high-level information. In pervasive computing, we emphasize the features and role of different information in different levels of personality.

(1) Low-level personal information is the directly sensed data about people, such as temperatures, accelerator readings, or records about human life, such as diaries and mails. Information of this level can be used as raw material to learn concepts and associated patterns of personal cognition, habits, attitudes, and thoughts. It can be used to infer mid/high-level personal information in a certain environment.

(2) Mid-level personal information is about concepts and concept patterns. A concept is something meaningful that has appeared in a person's life, It can be an event, an entity, an activity, facial expression, even a mood. Concepts can be inferred or recognized from low-level information, but cannot be sensed directly. For example, a group of people are having a conference and a person is showing a painful expression. With data at this level, we can integrate low-level data into meanings and can use this as an index to search related data and rules.

(3) High-level personal information is about experiences and intentions of people, representing knowledge about different concepts such as causality and dependency. Such relations are kept as the beliefs of people and can be used to infer user desires and plans, which are always an integral part of a user, including physical or psychological status.

Comparing the three levels, the lower level contains a larger amount of more concrete data but shows less structure and the higher level contains a smaller amount of more abstract data. The lower data is easier to gather, but the higher data reflects user motivations more exactly, as shown in Fig. 1.2.

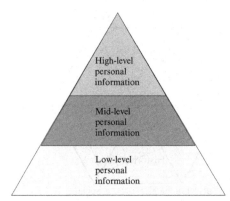

Inner fellings, affections, attitudes, motivations and psychological status

Actions, behaviors, gestures, situations, expressions, social relationships, events

Sensed physical data as temperature; sensed bodily data as heart rate; record data of people cognition as videos; body record as historial illness; historial physical data as statistics location data as GPS; social records as mails

Fig. 1.2 Three layers of personality

In cognitive frameworks such as the MIT Emotion Machine [25], personality data can be represented in six dimensions: temporal, spatial, physical, bodily, psychological, and social. An item of data information is represented as

$$\text{UserStatus} = (T, S, P, B, Psy, Sc) \tag{1.1}$$

We have made a conclusion about data content associated with the dimensions.

- *Temporal*: Records a time point or interval when personality information appeared in historical records or is scheduled to happen in the future.
- *Spatial*: Records a user's geographical location such as GPS data or logical location such as a block, a street, or a room; and objects nearby and the distances between them.
- *Physical*: Records sensed physical data such as temperature, humidity, light, and so on.
- *Bodily*: Records sensed body data such as heart rate, hormone level, and bioelectrical; body sensed data such as what a user sees, hears, smells, and touches; or body growth, injuries, and illnesses.
- *Psychological*: Records a user's feelings, mood, preference, and motivations.
- *Social*: Records a user's identity, career, economics, credit, and social relationships; such data can be stored in SNS, chats, messages, mails, and blogs.

We will introduce data models and management methods for each level, and information is measured with the dimensions.

1.4.1   Low-Level Personal Information

This model describes information sensed from sensors or obtained from files about users. We divided them into the following two categories: *instant sensed parameters* used for inference and *historical records* for analysis and learning, as shown in Fig. 1.3.

Fig. 1.3 Coverage of
low-level personal
information

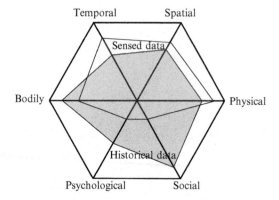

Instant sensed parameters are sensor data gathered directly by sensors, including ambient physical parameters, object physical parameters, bodily parameters, spatial parameters, and social parameters.

- Ambient physical parameters including temperature, light, sound, wind, humidity, gas, and chemicals, which directly affect people's feelings.
- Object physical parameters including speed, weight, height, parts, or materials which a user might use, such as a desk made of wood.
- Bodily parameters including user's acceleration, speed, strength, heart rate, body temperature, bioelectricity, breathing status, blood pressure, etc., to indicate the user's body status and which can be used to analyze the user's psychological status such as emotions or to predict an emergency, such as acute illness.
- Spatial parameters including user's geographical location such as GPS readings or logical locations such as a building or a street or GIS data; and related distance and positions of entities in space; also more structural descriptions about a location such as rooms in a building.
- Social parameters including one's instant communication via phone or network.

These kinds of data are generated without structure and changes frequently, needing efficient expression and management. Such data are enormous, heterogeneous, nonstandard, and hard to use directly, so before further processing, we must use different technologies to preprocess these data. We can reduce the data amount by sampling and using average or variance over time to substitute the raw data. We can rescale the sensor range to smooth the data diversity. We can also adopt sensor fusion techniques which aim at integrating the information from multiple sensors. There are three kinds of fusion: competitive fusion, complementary fusion, and cooperative fusion. Competitive fusion combines sensor data that represent the same measurement to reduce uncertainty and resolve conflicts. It is a basic fusion type. The fusion function always takes the form of weighting average. Complementary fusion combines incomplete sensor data not dependent on each other directly to create a more complete model. Cooperative fusion combines sensor observations that depend upon each other to deduce higher-level measurement. The commonly used sensor fusion methods include classical inference, Bayesian inference, Dempster–Shafer theory, voting and fuzzy logic. We adopt nature language processing techniques to analyse users' literal records, such as diaries or blogs to mine relative information.

Historical records are recorded files about previous data concerning personality, including the following issues:

- Cognition footprints that record what the user sees, hears, and smells, which can be used to mine the user's lifestyle and behavior.
- Ambient physical footprints that record historical ambient physical parameters about a group of environments related to a user, which can be used to analyze ambient physical features such as "in 308 sunny winter days in Hangzhou, 252 are very cold".
- Bodily footprints that record the historical body status of a person, such as medical records of illness, injury, fitness records, and diets.
- Spatial footprints that record the footprints of a user in different locations and can be used to analyze the moving habits of a person.
- Social footprints including record of a person's SNS, chats, messages, mails, and blogs, from which social relationships can be analyzed.

Such data can be either structural (SNS friend's lists, location records, mail lists, usefulness of applications) or nonstructural (mail content, blog dairies). It is complicated to make use of such data. Natural language processing (NLP) technologies can be used to analyze relations in plain text records; statistical learning methods can be used to learn about patterns of personality styles.

1.4.2 Mid-Level Personal Information

Mid-level personal information includes concepts with rich meaning about people's lives that can be inferred or recognized from low-level information. Concepts include, but are not limited to, such items as illustrated in Fig. 1.4:

- *Events*: Events happen in environments by accident, or some events happen as a direct consequence of behavior, such as when someone is drunk.
- *Behaviors*: Behavior is something the user is doing, such as reading, walking, drinking, and sleeping.
- *Situations*: Situations describe particular conditions of the environment or person. For example, a lot of people make up a crowd, "crowd" is a condition situation; working or entertainment are situations relating to user activities; when the boss came in, the office became nervous and serious; "nervous and serious" is a perceptual situation.
- *Emotions*: Emotions of users can be computed from body parameters or expression recognition.
- *Social Relationships*: Users' social relationships with others, e.g., friends, partners, teachers, etc.; or the changing of such relationships, which can be inferred from social footprints and events that happened between people.

Fig. 1.4 Coverage of
mid-level personal patterns

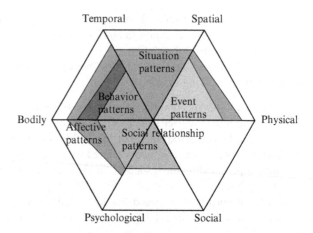

Concepts at this level can be expressed and learned as patterns or probability models. Patterns link nonstructural data to meaningful concepts. How to form a consistent pattern from raw characteristic data is broadly researched in many domains such as mathematics, psychology, ethology, linguistics, and cognitive science. Detecting a pattern and labeling a given concept is the main task of pattern recognition. Pattern recognition integrates many theories and algorithms of machine learning. Patterns can be detected and labeled as certain categories with both supervised learning and unsupervised learning. And a pattern can be used to analyze the low-level context of the environment and the reason for mid-level concepts with probability. Rich achievements in pattern recognition emerge in many disciplines.

Behavior recognition [26–29] and expression recognition [30, 31] take temporal body information such as acceleration or angular velocity and environmental physical information as the input to label unknown behavior according to different gestures, postures, and behavior. Similar algorithms can work in face and expression recognition. Face recognition helps to distinguish different people, and expression recognition helps to learn a person's attitudes and moods.

Affective computing [32, 33] integrates computer science with psychology, cognitive science, neuroscience, sociology, education, psychophysiology, ethics, and others. Affective computing learns about patterns that relate to and influence peoples' emotions. Many bodily and psychological techniques to assess frustration, stress and mood, are proposed.

Events are particularly important pieces of knowledge, since they represent activities of special significance for people, organizations, and environments. So event recognition [34] is of utmost importance in translating sensed data to knowledge. There are various aspects of event recognition, including analysis of video, audio, text, and other sensor data, as well as recognition of fused data sources and temporal reasoning systems. Situations [35] as a sequence pattern of time-stamped events

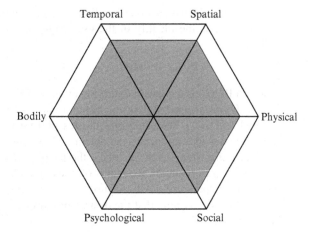

Fig. 1.5 Coverage of BDP

represent status of an entity, e.g., people or space. Both recognition of events and situations are adopted in many domains such as indoor environment monitoring, medical care, and others.

Social relationship patterns are researched by sociologists, cognitive scientists, psychologists, and computer scientists. Many models of social networks are being proposed. Data mining and behavior analysis [36] can be used to detect and classify social-related activities and relationships between communities and people in interaction, work, commerce, education, and everyday life.

1.4.3 High-Level Personal Information: BDP Model

High-level personal information describes the intention of people in different context states.

1.4.3.1 BDP Model

An important feature of SmartShadow is the ability to access an individual's personal needs and serve them automatically. A reasonable prerequisite for achieving this goal is to construct an intention model of users. Inspired by the BDI (Belief–Desire–Intention) agent model [37], we proposed a user intention model in an ubiquitous computing environment called BDP (Belief–Desire–Plan) model. The BDP model consists of three basic parts: beliefs, desires, and plans, as shown in Fig. 1.5.

(1) *Belief*: Belief is used to describe the users understanding of themselves (e.g., career, skill, health, and mood) and the world (e.g., cloudy sky implies rainfall),

and their attitude to the world (e.g., liking or hating). Belief is denoted as Bel_{uid}, in which uid is the identity of the user. Belief consists of a group of atomic beliefs:

$$\text{Bel}_{uid} = \text{Bel}(t_1, \ldots t_n) = \text{Bel}(t_1) \wedge \ldots, \wedge \text{Bel}(t_n) \qquad (1.2)$$

in which $\text{Bel}(t_i)$ is a concept definition or an assertion about concepts.

(2) *Desire*: Desire is used to describe instant requirements or motivations of users, denoted as Des_{uid}. We categorize desires into three types: (1) to accomplish specific tasks, such as "print a document"; (2) to make a specific object conform to a particular state, such as "make the room temperature come down to 25 degrees"; (3) to maintain the status of a specific object, such as "maintaining the room temperature". All concurrent desires of a user need to be logically compatible. We assume that the desires of a user can be inferred according to his beliefs.

(3) *Plan*: Plan is used to describe an action sequence for a user to accomplish his desire, denoted as Plan_{uid}. We define two types of plans: Primitive Plan, or Action, which describes an indivisible action to pursue a specific goal, such as calling a service; Composite Plan, which can be divided into a flow of subplans; a subplan can be either a Primitive or Composite Plan.

$$\text{Plan}_{uid} = \text{Plan}(t_1, \ldots t_n) = \text{Plan}(t_1) \wedge \ldots, \wedge \text{Plan}(t_n) \qquad (1.3)$$

A Composite Plan can be generated using three methods: executing a predefined action flow template; activating a subdesire and refining it in a hierarchy, such as HTN planning; or dynamically generating a plan with graph searching, as a graph-plan algorithm.

A BDP model is organized as a semantic network. A semantic network is a declarative graphic representation that can be used either to represent knowledge or to support automated systems for reasoning about knowledge. Some versions of a semantic network can be highly informal but other versions are formally defined systems of logic. There are six of the most common kinds of semantic networks [38]. BDP adopts a hybrid network representation which supports type inheritance, asserts propositions and implication of beliefs, causality, or inferences. BDP networks have been especially designed to support hypotheses about human cognitive mechanisms and facilitate computational inference for desires and plans.

1.4.3.2 Intention Evolution: From Belief to Plan

In a BDP model, beliefs of a person can trigger new desires under specific context conditions and a desire can generate a plan to execute. We call this procedure *Intention Evolution*, which can be divided into four stages (Fig. 1.6):

(1) *Belief Revision*: According to gathered context information, related belief states are modified. At the same time, new assertions are learned about context and cognitive knowledge and the belief set is updated.

Fig. 1.6 Intention
evolvement in the BDP
model

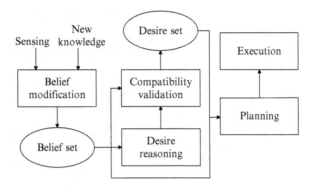

(2) *Desire Reasoning and Validation*: Firstly, this takes context states from the belief set as facts and takes cognitive assertions from the belief set as rules about personal requirements under different context conditions. Secondly, this determines whether the generated desires are feasible in the current context situation and whether the new desires are compatible with other desires in the desire set. If true, they will be added to the desire set.

(3) *Planning*: According to the user's context, a suitable plan is generated for each desire in the desire set.

(4) *Execution*: Executing subplans in turn. Primitive plans are invoked directly and the composite plan will produce a sequence of subplans to be executed sequentially. For efficiency and reliability, the execution process revises itself according to changes in the user's desires and context information, to select a better service, achieve fault tolerance, and prevent senseless execution. The execution of primitive plans is rather simple; the execution algorithm for composite plans is shown in Fig. 1.7.

One composite plan dynamically searches for a subplan at runtime and generates an execution tree, in which primitive plans are leaf nodes. An initial plan is recursively expanded to more detailed subplans during execution. An execution tree need not be fully expanded with all subplans executed. In contrast, once a user believes his desire is satisfied, the execution succeeds and stops. However, if the plan can find a better subplan or if a subplan fails, it needs to replan for a new plan. If replanning cannot find any plans to resume a failed execution, the desire of the initial plan has failed.

1.5   Modeling Computing Environments

A smart environment is the space where user tasks are carried out, consisting of networked software and hardware connected to the physical world. It provides functionalities to complete user tasks and meet users' requirements. Semantic representation of a smart environment is necessary to achieve automation of task

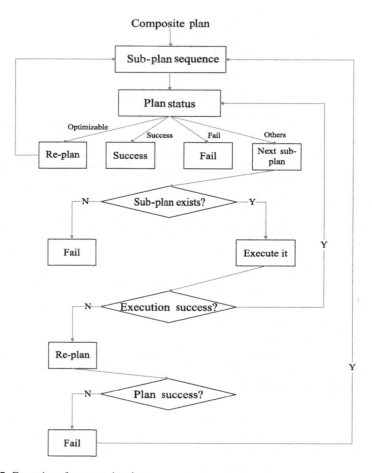

Fig. 1.7 Execution of a composite plan

migration [15]. Services and devices can be regarded as the two most important kinds of entities in a smart environment. Services characterize not only software functionalities but also parts of hardware functionalities in smart environments. Devices provide the computing environments for services. In this book, we refer to devices in a more generic sense, as general appliances or facilities besides computing devices. Moreover, users and contexts in an environment are two factors in the dynamic characteristics of the environment. They are both critical in building a ServiceShadow. Similar to the description of people information, we use the ontology technology to semantically describe a smart environment, including entries of service, device, user and environment context, depicted in Fig. 1.8 [11]. As the environment context has been widely researched, e.g., the context ontology proposed by Preuveneers, here we briefly introduce the other three.

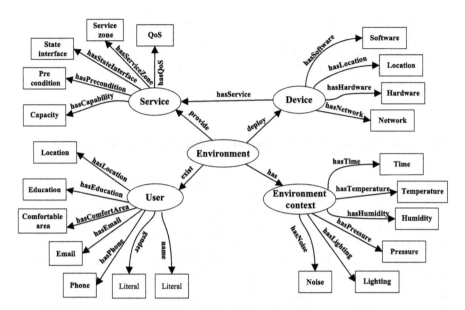

Fig. 1.8 Ontology for an environment (in part)

(1) *Service*: Here the term service includes not only information services (such as media data processing, and document editing) but also device services (such as light control, and printing). Note that web services belong to information services. Service description is achieved in terms of Capability, QoS, Preconditions, ServiceZone, and StateInterface. The Capability and QoS specify the functional and nonfunctional properties of a service; the ServiceZone specifies the effective range of a service, which is defined with Zone Ontology; the Precondition describes the context constraints of this service and is formalized by the first-order predicate PRE; State-Interface describes state interfaces and is defined with data type description and ServiceState. The ServiceState represents the states supported by the service and defined by the State Ontology, which is formalized in the same way as InternalState TS.

(2) *Device*: Devices are the container of information services and provide device services for users. It is impossible for service developers to know the detailed information on the deployment of a service in advance. Therefore, device description can be complementary to service description. Device description is defined in terms of service, location, hardware, software, and network. The service represents the services deployed on the device, with reference to service ontology. The location represents the deployment location of the device, which is difficult to specify in the service description. The hardware, software, and network represent the underlying details about this device.

(3) *User*: User description is a key step to achieve adaption and smartness in the user-centric computing environment. We define the user description based

on the person ontology of SOUPA, which specifies a personal profile of a user, including identity, name, location, gender, education, and intentions. The user description also specifies a comfortable interaction zone. Only within this range is a user comfortable with the moving distance to interact with some services/devices.

1.6 Planning for a Virtual Service Space: ServiceShadow

Once the intentions of a user and the services in the environment are known, a virtual service space can be constructed with service discovery, matching, and composition by a planning algorithm. In planning, an intention of a user is embodied in a service flow that composes a sequence of environmental services. A planning problem is always described in a five-tuple with the form of $< S, S_0, G, A, \Gamma >$. In this five-tuple, set S represents all possible states in a user's task; S_0, a subset of S, contains the legal initial states of the user's task; G is another subset of S with the legal goal states of the task. A represents the actions that can be carried out currently by the system and Γ contains the state functions of actions in A; an action can transform a precondition s_1 to an effect condition s_2. A planner takes such five-tuples as input parameters. It is convenient to convert the desired models and service models into planning problems, because the preconditions and desired results of an atomic task are specified in its description. An action can be mapped to a service, with its preconditions and effects as a function of status change that can be extracted directly from the ontology models.

A planning algorithm is similar to finding an optimal path from an initial state to a goal state. An example is shown in Fig.1.9. In the figure, we want to transform current world state (initial state) to a certain goal state. The transformation has two intermediate states: *state 1* and *state 2*. Several services can lead a state to another. The cost to invoke service j after service i is marked as $Cost(i, j)$ that is represented as an edge. The planning needs to find a path from initial state to goal state with minimal total cost.

Considering the similarity of our ontology models and the Planning Domain Definition Language (PDDL) [40], PDDL is widely accepted as a standardized input by many planners. We can express our planning problems in PDDL and generate the *service* flow with a planner. If an action can be achieved by multiple services, we need a matching process to find an optimized service flow so we have also proposed a semantic-based task-to-service mapping algorithm to filter services with compatibility of context and functionalities with a satisfaction measurement according to service capability, locality, and QoS to find the best services.

In a dynamic environment, users and services always move to a different place and suffer changing context conditions when motivation or context changes. ServiceShadow may need to be revised time after time, due to many reasons such as service unavailability, service QoS changing, users goals changing, occurrence of better services, etc. A service flow is analogous to a business activity in Web Service

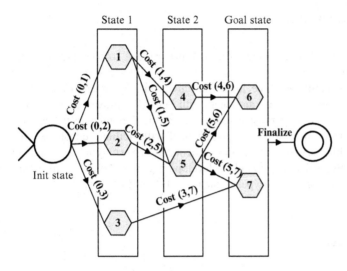

Fig. 1.9 An exmaple for planning algorithm

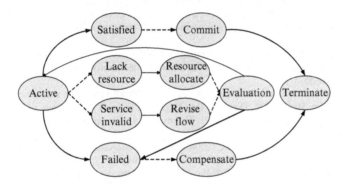

Fig. 1.10 An adaptation strategy

but it has more states and personalized context-aware state transition conditions. In addition, a task doesn't need to be roll-backed or compensated when something happens, but, as mentioned before, it needs to continue until either the user goal is fulfilled or canceled or the planner cannot generate an alternative service flow. If the resource of a service becomes insufficient due to competition or context effect, at that time ServiceShadow is responsible for allocating resources such as data caches, network bandwidth for that service. If a required service will leave, the ServiceShadow needs to be re-planned. Re-planning takes the current step as the start state of the planning algorithm to update the affected part of service flow, which might lead to migration to an alternative service or lead to a totally distinct service flow. An adaptation strategy is shown in Fig. 1.10.

1.7   Conclusion

We have built SmartShadow, a user-centric model, to characterize the properties and capabilities of user personality and a mobile virtual user space. By modeling users' personality on three levels, an environment can learn and analyze users' lifestyle, beliefs, desires, and plan with sensed contexts; and by modeling the environment, users' pervasive services could be dynamically filtered and mapped into the virtual user space. A good model will facilitate developers to construct more flexible pervasive computing systems. We are studying the application of the proposed SmartShadow model in developing generic software infrastructures and are deploying some prototypes in the real world to further verify the model.

References

1. Weiser M (1991) The computer for the 21st century. Sci Am 265(3):66–75
2. Wu Z H, Pan G (2006) Pervasive computing. Proceedings of China computer federation (CCFP-0002). Tsinghua University Press, Beijing, pp 175–187 (in Chinese)
3. Dima A, Ciarletta L (2000) A conceptual model for pervasive computing. In: Sadayappan P (ed) Proceedings of IEEE international workshops on parallel processing. IEEE Press, Toronto, pp 9–15
4. Muhlhauser M (2000) Ubiquitous computing and its influence on MSE. In: Denise Williams A (ed) Proceedings of international symposium on multimedia software engineering, IEEE Press, Taipei, pp 48–55
5. Henricksen K, Indulska J, Rakotonirainy A (2001) Infrastructure for pervasive computing: challenges. In: Stefani J-B, Demeure IM, Hagimont D (eds) Proceedings of workshop on pervasive computing INFORMATIK 01, Osterreichische Computer Gesellschaft, Vienna, pp 214–222
6. Xu GY, Tao LM, Zhang DP, Shi YC (2006) The dual relationship between physical space and information space. Chin Sci Bull 51(5):610–616 (in Chinese)
7. Ranganathan A, Campbell RH (2008) Provably correct pervasive computing environments. In: Werner B (ed) Proceedings of the sixth annual IEEE international conference on pervasive computing and communications, IEEE Press, Hong Kong, pp 160–169
8. de Deugd S, Carroll R, Kelly KE, Millett B, Ricker J (2006) SODA: service-oriented device architecture. IEEE Pervasive Comput 5(3):94–96
9. Costa C, Yamin A, Geyer C (2008) Toward a general software infrastructure for ubiquitous computing. IEEE Pervasive Comput 7(1):64–73
10. Zhang L, Pan G, Wu ZH, Li SJ, Wang CL (2009) SmartShadow: modeling a user-centric mobile virtual space. In: Proceedings of 7th IEEE international conference on pervasive computing and communications (PerCom'09), Galveston, TX
11. Pan G, Xu YQ, Wu ZH, Yang L, Lin M, Li SJ, Liu Z (2011) TaskShadow: towards seamless task migration across smart environments. IEEE Intel Syst 26(3):50–57
12. Neurath O, Carnap R, Morris CFW (eds) (1955) International encyclopedia of unified science. University of Chicago Press, Chicago
13. Berners-Lee T, Hendler J, Lassila O (2001) The semantic web. Sci Am 284(5):34–43
14. Eric JM (2001) An introduction to the resource description framework. J Libr Adm 34(3):245–255
15. Maja H, Pornpit W, Tharam D, Elizabeth C (2009) Introduction to ontology. Ontol Based Multi-Agent Syst 219:37–60

16. Renzo A, Claudio G (2008) The expressive power of SPARQL. In: Sheth AP, Staab S, Dean M, Paolucci M, Maynard D, Finin TW, Thirunarayan K (eds) Proceedings of the 7th international conference on the semantic web (ISWC'08), Karlsruhe. Springer, pp 114–129
17. Hazaël-Massieux D, Connolly D (2004) Gleaning resource descriptions from dialects of languages (GRDDL). World Wide Web Consortium, W3C Coordination Group Note, NOTE-grddl-20040413, 2004. http://www.w3.org/TR/grddl/
18. Jeremy JC, Christian B, Pat H, Patrick S (2005) Named graphs, provenanace and trust. In: Ellis A (ed) Proceedings of the 14th international conference on World Wide Web (WWW'05), Chiba. ACM, pp 613–622
19. Chen H, Finin T, Joshi A (2004) Semantic web in the context broker architecture. In: Proceedings of the second IEEE international conference on pervasive computing and communications, pp 277–286
20. Strang T, Linnho-Popien C, Frank K (2003) CoOL: a context ontology language to enable contextual interoperability. In: Bauknecht K, Brauer W, Mück TA (eds) Proceedings of 4th IFIP international conference on distributed applications and interoperable systems, Springer, Heidelberg, pp 236–247
21. Wang XH, Zhang DQ, Gu T, Pung HK (2004). Ontology based context modeling and reasoning using OWL. In: Werner B (ed) Proceedings of the second IEEE annual conference on pervasive computing and communications workshops, IEEE Press, pp 18–22
22. Chen H, Perich F, Finin T, Joshi A (2004) SOUPA: standard ontology for ubiquitous and pervasive applications. In: Frances MT (ed) Proceedings of first annual international conference on mobile and ubiquitous systems, IEEE Press, pp 258–267
23. Lehmann O, Bauer M, Becker C, Nicklas D (2004) From home to world-supporting context-aware applications through world models. Proceedings of the second IEEE annual conference on pervasive computing and communications, pp 297–306
24. von Eckardt B (2006) Cognitive science: philosophical issues. In: Nadel L (ed) Encyclopedia of cognitive science. Nature Publishing, London, pp 552–559
25. Push S (2005) EM-ONE: an architecture for reflective commonsense thinking. PhD thesis, MIT
26. Bao L, Intille, S (2004) Activity recognition from user-annotated acceleration data. In: Ferscha A, Mattern F (eds) International conference on pervasive computing (Pervasive'04), Springer, pp 1–17
27. Wu JH, Pan G, Zhang DQ, Qi GD, Li SJ (2009) Gesture recognition with a 3D accelerometer. The 6th international conference on ubiquitous intelligence and computing (UIC'09), Brisbane, Australia, 7–9 July 2009
28. Pan G, Zhang Y, Wu Z (2009) Accelerometer-based gait recognition via voting by signature points. Electron Lett 45(22):1116–1118
29. Pan G, Wu J, Zhang D, Wu Z, Yang Y, Li S (2010) GeeAir: a universal multimodal remote control device for home appliances. Pers Ubiquitous Comput 14(8):723–735
30. Caifeng S, Shaogang G, Peter WM (2009) Facial expression recognition based on local binary patterns: a comprehensive study. Image Vis Comput 27(6):803–816
31. Cohen I, Sebe N, Chen L, Garg A, Huang TS (2003) Facial expression recognition from video sequences: temporal and static modeling. Comput Vis Image Underst (CVIU) 91:160–187
32. Tao JH, Tan TN (2005) Affective computing: a review. Affect Comput Intell Interact 3784:981–995
33. Rosalind WP (2003) Affective computing: challenges. Int J Hum-Comput Stud 59(1–2):55–64
34. Johnson N, Hogg D (1996) Learning the distribution of object trajectories for event recognition. Image Vis Comput 14(8):609–615
35. Dousson C, Gaborit P, Ghallab M (1993) Situation recognition: representation and algorithms. In: Bajcsy R (ed) Proceedings of the 13th international joint conference on artificial intelligence (IJCAI'93). Morgan Kaufmann, San Francisco, CA, pp 166–172
36. Eagle N, Pentland A (2009) Reality mining: sensing complex social systems. Pers Ubiquitous Comput 10(4):255–268

37. Rao AS, Georgeff MP (1991) Modeling rational agents within a BDI-architecture. In: Allen J, Fikes R, Sandewall E (eds) Proceedings of the 2nd international conference on principles of knowledge representation and reasoning, Morgan Kaufmann, San Francisco, CA, pp 473–484
38. Sowa JF (1992) Conceptual graphs as a universal knowledge representation. Comput Math Appl 23(2–5):75–93
39. Pan G, Li Z, Li S, Wu Z (2009) SmartShadow: a model of pervasive computing. J Softw 20(S1):40–50 (in Chinese)
40. Fox M, Long D (2003) Pddl2.1: An extension to Pddl for expressing temporal planning domains. J Artif Intell Res 20:61–124

Chapter 2
Task Migration in SmartShadow

Abstract In everyday life, users frequently move across various environments. User mobility poses a great challenge for SmartShadow to seamlessly migrate users' tasks, which requires tasks to follow users continuously and seamlessly. This chapter proposes a scheme for seamless task migration. A task model and a semantic representation of smart environments enabling task migration are introduced. Given the requirements of tasks and capabilities of environments, we propose a task-to-service mapping algorithm to semantically search for suitable low-level services that achieve high-level tasks. The SmartShadow also defines a mechanism to measure user satisfaction.

2.1 Introduction

The emergence of pervasive computing paradigm envisions a smart world in which people can achieve their tasks and realize their intentions in a smart and unobtrusive manner. Someday, enormous commodities with the capabilities of sensing or actuating will be ubiquitously deployed in smart environments. It is desirable that users are able to move hand-free across various smart environments yet make use of local commodities of environments to continue their ongoing tasks anytime. In such smart environments, tasks will be involved not only in computational devices, such as desktop computers, printers, and smart phones, but also in various controllable facilities deployed in local physical environments, such as doors, curtains, and coffeemakers.

Figure 2.1 illustrates user mobility across smart environments such as office, home, and car.

It is still a big challenge to make tasks follow people in a seamless way, suffering from the environment's dynamics, the system's heterogeneity, the user's mobility, and the task's abstractness. Seamless task migration is crucial to achieve

Z. Wu and G. Pan, *SmartShadow: Models and Methods for Pervasive Computing*, Advanced Topics in Science and Technology in China, DOI 10.1007/978-3-642-36382-5_2, © Zhejiang University Press, Hangzhou and Springer-Verlag Berlin Heidelberg 2013

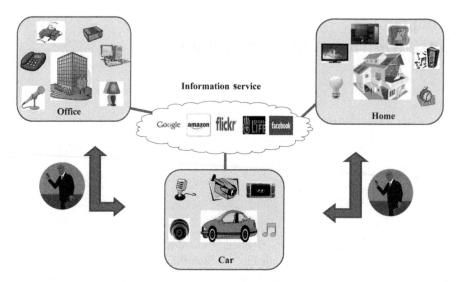

Fig. 2.1 Illustration of user mobility across smart environments

"user-centricity," the ultimate goal of pervasive computing. It is drawing more and more attention from the researchers in the pervasive computing community. A task is a specific piece of a user's work required to be done. The reasons for task migration are mainly twofold. Firstly, the execution of a task requires interaction with the user, i.e., a task cannot be finished in a silent manner. Secondly, a task requires local devices and commodities of a smart environment to fulfill the user's requirements. Currently, users are usually involved in many efforts to manually configure systems to continue the ongoing tasks when they move to a new environment. Although service-oriented computing is widely used as a paradigm to develop the pervasive computing infrastructure and also has been explored to tackle user mobility and task migration for its loosely coupling and dynamic composition [1–3], it is far from seamless task migration because of the semantic gap between tasks and services. "Task" is a high-level and user-oriented term, which is associated with the user's requirements, while "service" is a low-level and system-oriented term, which is associated with system functionalities.

This chapter describes a taskshadow framework [4] toward seamless task migration. In this framework, a petri-net-based task model is proposed for modeling both task process and internal states, describing a task as a coalition of primitive tasks. With the help of semantic awareness and the task model, when a user moves from one space to another, a context-aware task-to-service mapping approach will automatically find the most suitable services in the new space, and then seamlessly restore the states of the unfinished primitive tasks to resume user tasks.

2.2 Related Work

In the Aura project, Wang and Garlan [3] describe a paradigm of task-driven computing, which focuses on computation. A unit of abstract functionality is represented by a virtual service. A task is regarded as a top-level virtual service that may be decomposed into a set of virtual services. Thus a task can be achieved by executing its virtual services that are bound to physical services. The Aura project has no semantic modeling of tasks, services, and devices, which makes it difficult in context-adaptive matching services in an open manner to continue a user task.

In the Amigo project [2,5], a user task is described as an abstract OWL-S process with no reference to existing services, and each environment's service is described as a Semantic Web Service with a conversation. A two-step semantic matching algorithm is presented to compose the conversation of an abstract user task using fragments of the available services in the environment. However, it does not address the task recovery issue when a user moves from one place to another.

In the Gaia project [6], application mobility in active spaces is addressed. From the development viewpoint, a Model-View-Controller-based application framework is proposed to support both intra-space and inter-space mobility. It models applications as a set of distributed components, which can be duplicated and moved to different resources contained in an active space. The Gaia OS is provided as system software infrastructure to implement mobility. Gaia's scheme is a tight coupling solution for mobility, which cannot cope with openness and heterogeneity of smart environments.

Preuveneers and Berbers [7] use the OSGi platform to implement the smart service's synchronization. They mainly focus on service diffusion and how to redeploy the same service on other hosts in a synchronous service state. The approach cannot deal with high-level task migration across heterogeneous devices since it has no semantic abstraction of tasks and environments.

MDAgent [8, 9] exploits the use of software agents to support application-level mobility. They solve the problem of application mobility from the aspects of the underlying application model, mobility management, collaboration of different kinds of software agents, resource matching. However, MDAgent cannot also deal with high-level task migration across heterogeneous devices.

Satyanarayanan et al. [10] describe a system-level strategy toward seamless mobility for computing hardware in desktop computing environments, named the ISR (Internet Suspend/Resume) mechanism. It encapsulates the entire state of a personal computer and delivers it anywhere as requested. ISR just focuses on desktop computing mobility and does not concern itself with semantic issues and distributed issues caused by migration over an open infrastructure.

Our previous work, called ScudOSGi [11], enables facility-involved task migration that focuses on how to maximize usage of local facilities for user tasks. It proposes a two-level application model to simplify development of applications supporting migration and semantic descriptions of tasks and devices to rebind devices after the user. However, the proposed semantic descriptions are simple and incomplete.

2.3 Task Migration Challenges

Task migration enables a task to follow a user as if the task is the user's shadow. The most important requirement of task migration is seamlessness, which has continuity and is intervention-free. Continuity means the user should have a continual experience of task transition from one place to another. Intervention-free means very little user attention is needed even if a task may involve many devices. The main challenges are from:

(1) Abstractness: User tasks are high-level and usually abstract, which are required to be interpreted and matched in the current space (environment) correctly before task execution.
(2) Mobility: In smart environments, the user's mobility is frequent and sometime random, which causes task disruption and thus task recovery is necessary.
(3) Heterogeneity: Smart environments usually have a variety of different scales of devices, different hardware, different software platforms, and different network types.
(4) Dynamicity: The contexts of environments may vary with time.
    To counter the above challenges toward seamless task migration across smart environments, we make the following efforts:

• Adopt both semantic-based and process-based task model to enable task migration. A task model is used to represent and interpret an abstract task, so that systems can understand the requirements and intents of a user. Moreover, in order to support task continuity when the user moves, the task model is able to model the real-time state of tasks.
• Task-to-Service Mapping. Tasks are actually accomplished by collaboration of entities in smart environments. Mapping from task to service helps to bridge the gap between user's requirements and system functionalities. It should select a series of appropriate services to start/resume a task while meeting the user's satisfaction as much as possible.

2.3.1 Scenario: Watching Movie

A simple scenario of task migration is "watching movie." Tom's father is driving home in the afternoon, while Tom is watching the latest movie in the car with the in-car speaker and mini-display. When they arrive home, the movie is not over yet. Tom hopes to continue watching the movie at home. When he enters the house and sits down in the living room, the movie resumes playing on the LCD-TV opposite to Tom. The hi-fi speaker in the living room, Tom's favorite, is automatically opened and tuned at a comfortable volume. Meanwhile, the curtains of living room are closed, which could darken the environment and enhance the effect of the movie's playing.

2.4 Task Model in SmartShadow

Task is an abstract concept. It describes user's intents and requirements. A task model should be independent on environments and users. We assume that a task is a cooperation of a series of primitive tasks, which means a task can be decomposed to primitive tasks. This assumption was also adopted in the Aura project [4].

To enable seamless task migration, a task model should represent not only the relationship among the primitive tasks of a task but also the state of the tasks. The task state should include:

(1) The status of task process: When a task migration occurs, we should know which primitive tasks should be processed immediately and which primitive tasks have been completed and should not be processed again to avoid duplication.
(2) The internal state of primitive tasks: When a user moves, it is possible that some primitive task has started but has not been completed yet. Thus the internal state needs to be saved to achieve task continuity.

Therefore, we model a task from two aspects, the task process and the semantic description of primitive tasks. The task process describes the processing flow of the primitive tasks in a task and guarantees the global continuity of the task, whose model is based on Petri-net; the semantic description represents the semantic information of a primitive task and supports the internal state, which is modeled based on ontology.

2.4.1 Modeling Task Process

The task process describes the relationship among the primitive tasks of a task. Since Petri-net [12] has powerful ability to represent a concurrent process both mathematically and conceptually, we employ it to model the task process. Meanwhile, in order to achieve task continuity, a task-status set is introduced into Petri-net to be able to track the status of each primitive task.

A Task Petri-Net (TPN) for the task process is represented by a six-tuple:

$$\text{TPN} = < P, T, F, M, G, S >$$

- P is a finite set of places, which represent the primitive tasks in the TPN. There is one special primitive task named "End" representing the end of the task.
- T is a finite set of transition with $P \cup T = \emptyset$, which represents different stages of the task.
- $F \subseteq (P \times T) \cup (T \times P)$ is the flow relation, which represents the relationship between primitive tasks.
- M is a function that associates the number of tokens with each place in the net, which is zero or one in the TPN. The place with one token means the primitive task it represented can be activated, namely, the primitive task can be carried out by an actual service immediately.
- G is a guard function, mapping a Boolean expression to each transition, which is used to judge whether the next primitive task can be activated or not.
- S is a function that associates places to the task-status set, which represents the status of the associated primitive tasks. The task-status set is specified as

$$\{Completed, Processing, Unstartted, Paused\}$$

where "*Completed*" represents primitive tasks that have already been completed; "*Processing*" represents primitive tasks beginning to be executed; *Unstarted* represents primitive tasks that have not started yet; and "*Paused*" represents primitive tasks that have started and are not completed yet.

In the TPN, the initial status of the primitive tasks is all "*Unstarted.*" When the guard function associated with the transition is satisfied, the transition will fire, which means the next primitive task(s) can be activated. If there are appropriate services for the activated primitive tasks, then their status will become "*Processing.*" After the primitive tasks are completed, their status will become "*Completed.*" When the "End" task is activated, the task represented by the TPN is completed.

By using the TPN, we can determine which primitive tasks should continue to be executed when the user leaves for a new environment:

(1) When a user leaves a space, the status of the primitive tasks will be saved immediately: If the status of primitive task is "*Completed*" or "*Unstarted,*" its status will be saved directly; if the status is "*Processing,*" its status will be changed to "*Paused*" and saved.
(2) When a user enters a new environment, the task should follow him or her. This can be done by resuming the saved TPN: For the primitive tasks whose status is "*Complete,*" they will be omitted to avoid re-executing. For the primitive tasks whose status is "*Unstarted,*" they will be checked as to whether they can be activated and executed in the new environment. For the primitive task whose status is "*Paused,*" they will be resumed from the saved internal state if the state exists. Otherwise, they will be executed like "*Unstarted*" status.

In addition, the TPN model has the capability to describe if a primitive task in a TPN is optional or mandatory. A primitive task is optional in a TPN if it has no flow to the "End" task. Otherwise, it is mandatory. This feature allows the tasks to be completed even if there are no local facilities in a smart environment to complete those optional primitive tasks.

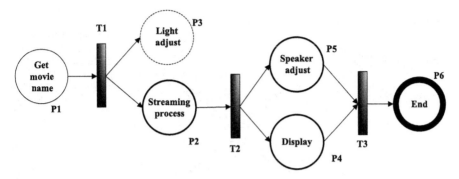

Fig. 2.2 Task Petri-Net of "watch movie" (Color figure online)

Figure 2.2 shows the TPN of the "watching movie" task consisting of six primitive tasks, which are "Get Movie Name", "Streaming Process," "Light Adjust," "Speaker Adjust," "Display," and "End" primitive tasks. The "Light Adjust" is optional (no flows to "End"), since the watching movie task can resume without completion of the "Light Adjust." Assume that a user leaves a car, the status of primitive tasks may be as follows: "Get Movie Name" is *Completed* (shown as green circles in the figure), "Light Adjust" (no local appliance to complete it in the car) and "End" are "*Unstarted*" (in white), and the rest of the primitive tasks are "*Paused*" (in red).

2.4.2 Describing a Primitive Task

TPN supports interpretation of the task process and guarantees the continuity of tasks. However, how should we interpret and represent primitive tasks so that they can be interpreted and completed in heterogeneous smart environments? Semantic representation of primitive tasks will further describe primitive tasks in TPN.

We employ ontology [13] to establish a primitive task description, depicted in Fig. 2.3. The information on *Functionality* and *NonFunctionality* is determined before the task is instantiated. *Functionality* specifies functional requirements of a primitive task, and is described in terms of *Functionality type*, *Input*, and *Output*, which can be defined by external related ontologies. *NonFunctionality* specifies nonfunctional requirements, including *Security*, *Performance*, and *Cost*, which are defined based on the QoS model by Liu and Issarny [14]. The other two components, *Owner* and *InternalState*, are valid only after a primitive task is instantiated. *Owner* specifies personal information about the task owner and is with reference to a user model. The *InternalState* specifies the internal states and is defined with the state ontology.

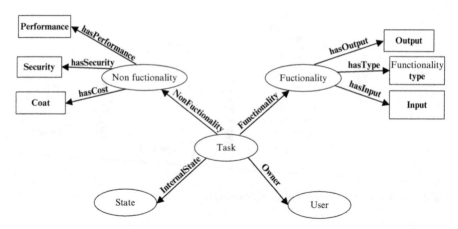

Fig. 2.3 Ontology for a primitive task (in part)

To describe the semantic information of a task more directly and conveniently, we introduce the formalized representation of the primitive task t in the TPN:

$$t =< U, F_t, NF_t, TS >,$$

where U is the user who hopes to execute primitive task t; F_t is the required functionality set of primitive task t. It is specified by $< I_t, O_t, FT_t >$, where I_t, O_t, and FT_t respectively represent the Input, Output, and Functionality Type Ontology required by t. NF_t is the nonfunctionality requirement set of primitive task t. TS is the internal state of primitive task t, it is specified by $\{\tau_1, \cdots, \tau_k\}$, where τ_i represents the semantic description of the ith internal state with State Ontology.

2.5   Context-Aware Task-to-Service Mapping

Using the task model, we can interpret the requirements of a task in detail. Using the semantic representation of a smart environment (for details refer to Chap. 2), we can abstract the capabilities and characteristics of a smart environment in terms of service, device, environment context, and user, shielding the underlying implementation. However, there still lacks a bridge to connect them.

Our task-to-service mapping algorithm gives a framework to connect user-side tasks and system-side services. Given the TPN of a task, the task-to-service mapping is for finding the best matched services from the local environment for each of the uncompleted primitive tasks to resume an ongoing task. Figure 2.4 shows a task-to-service mapping example of "watching movie." When a user moves from car to home, different services are dynamically organized for the primitive tasks in the TPN for task continuity.

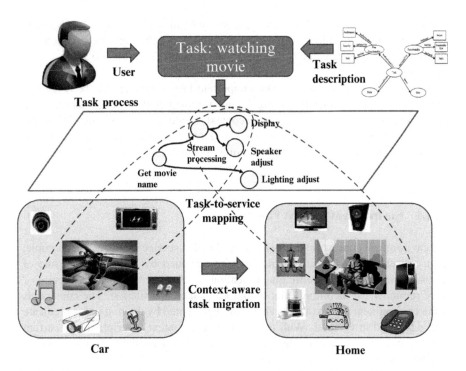

Fig. 2.4 Context-aware task-to-service mapping: an example of "watching movie"

In order to reduce the complexity of the mapping, we construct the algorithm in two steps:

(1) Semantic service filtering: It filters the services that do not meet the specific requirements of the primitive task t, including functionality requirement, and context constraints (e.g., environment, task, and user contexts). The screened services will all satisfy the requirements of the primitive task t, and serve as the candidates for the next step.
(2) Task-oriented service matching: This step is to improve the seamless experience and satisfaction of users for task migration. It optimally selects the best-matched service for t. We define three satisfaction measures as a goal function for optimal matching.

2.5.1 Semantic Service Filtering

When the total number of services available in the smart environment becomes large, service matching may take a lot of time. To reduce the time overhead in the service matching step, we filter those improper services. At first, we use functionality type FT to filter the services that do not meet the functionality requirement of the primitive task, called Functionality Filtering. The functionality filtering can be carried out by an index mechanism (functionality-type FT as the key).

Besides functionality, there are two important factors that need to be taken into account for seamless task migration: (1) environment context: those services that are not able to adapt to the environment context should be screened out. (2) internal state of the paused task: To achieve task continuity, the selected services should be compatible with the saved task state, if required, which further limits the candidates of matched services.

2.5.1.1 Environment Context Filtering

The environment context is usually closely related to service usability. For example, when a user is at a meeting (which can be reasoned by using the schedule of the user combined with the time and location of the environment), the service of voice reminder for incoming calls should be banned and filtered. The constraints of the environment context for service s are represented by the first-order predicate PRE described in Chap. 2. With the environment context description, the current environment context can be reasoned using predicate logic defined in the PRE to determine whether a service is suitable or not.

2.5.1.2 Task State Filtering

Primitive tasks may be involved in the recovery of the internal task state in the "to" environment, which requires the primitive-task-specific state recovery capability of services to support task migration. Task state filtering will determine whether a service can support and handle the state recovery for the primitive task.

Assume that the internal state of a primitive task t is represented as TS_t, and the state supported by the service s is represented as SS_s, as described in Sect. 2.4.2. We want to know whether SS_s is compatible with TS_t saved in t, which is defined by state ontology. This problem is equal to identifying semantic relationships between ontology concepts. In our scheme, the classic Subsumption Relationship Algorithm proposed by Paolucci et al. [15] is employed. The compatible constraint between t and s can be evaluated by the following equation:

$$\text{Compatible}(t,s) \equiv \forall \tau_i \in TS_t, \ \exists \tau_j \in SS_s \cdot \text{subsume}(\tau_i, \tau_j) \tag{2.1}$$

where $\text{subsume}(\tau_i, \tau_j)$ equals to TRUE if the concept τ_j subsumes τ_i. If t and s satisfy the compatible constraint, then s can recover the internal state of t; otherwise, s will be filtered.

2.5.2 Satisfaction Measurement for Task-Oriented Matching

Each of the resulting services after semantic service filtering is able to complete the primitive task. However, the services are different in providing user experiences. Some are convenient to use and agree with user preference, some may be not. Task-oriented matching will find the most suitable service from the candidates to provide the best user satisfaction of task migration. We consider three factors for the satisfaction Ψ of mapping service s to task t:

$$\Psi(t,s) = \alpha_1 \times \Psi_C(t,s) + \alpha_2 \times \Psi_L(t,s) + \alpha_3 \times \Psi_Q(t,s) \qquad (2.2)$$

where $\Psi_C(t,s)$ is the capability satisfaction, $\Psi_L(t,s)$ is the locality satisfaction, $\Psi_Q(t,s)$ is the QoS satisfaction, and α_1, α_2, α_3 are the weight coefficients with $\alpha_1 + \alpha_2 + \alpha_3 = 1$.

2.5.2.1 Capability Satisfaction

The candidate services generated by Functionality Filtering meet the functional requirement of the current primitive task. However, they satisfy a user to different degrees. For example, for the "watch movie" task with AVI format file as input, the streaming processing service designed specifically for AVI format will be better than the general streaming processing service. We define the degree of satisfaction between functionality provided by s and capability required by t, namely, the Capability Satisfaction, as

$$\Psi_Q(t,s) = \text{Sim}(I_t, I_s) \times \text{Sim}(O_t, O_s) \qquad (2.3)$$

where I_t and O_t are the input and output capability of task t, described by ontology. I_s and O_s are the input and output of service s, described by ontology; $\text{Sim}(\cdot, \cdot)$ means semantic similarity. To compute $\text{Sim}(\cdot, \cdot)$, we firstly analyze the subsumption relationship between the two concepts by the classic Subsumption Relationship Algorithm and then apply the following equation:

$$\text{Sim}(O_1, O_2) = \begin{cases} 1 - \frac{|\text{Level}(O_1) - \text{Level}(O_2)|}{\text{Total level of ontology}} & \text{if subsume}(O_1, O_2) \text{ or subsume}(O_2, O_1) \\ 0 & \text{Otherwise} \end{cases}$$

$$(2.4)$$

2.5.2.2 Locality Satisfaction

When selecting local devices, locality is an important factor that affects user satisfaction. Here, the locality has two meanings: (1) Service Zone: When the distance between the user and the service is beyond the Service Zone, this service is useless for completion of the user task. For example, when a user and printer service are not in the same environment (beyond the Service Zone of the printer service), the printer service cannot effectively help the completion of the user's printing task; (2) Comfortable Distance for Interaction: Users generally prefer to use the interaction devices in the vicinity for their tasks.

We define locality satisfaction for enhancing user experience regarding locality, which is a function of the comfortable zone for interaction Z_u, location of the user L_u, service zone Z_s, and location of the service L_s:

$$\Psi_L(t,s) = \phi(Z_u, Z_s, L_u, L_s) = \begin{cases} 1 & \text{if } L_s \in Z_u \\ 0 & \text{if } L_s \notin Z_u \\ \beta_1 \times \frac{L_{far} - L_{dis}}{L_{far}} + \beta_2 \times \cos\theta & \text{Otherwise} \end{cases} \quad (2.5)$$

where L_{far} is the maximum distance from a location in the zone $Z_s | Z_u$ into the comfortable zone Z_u; L_{dis} is the distance when a user moves from L_u to L_s; θ is the angle between the user facing direction and the vector $L_u L_s$; β_1, β_2 are weight coefficients, $\beta_1 + \beta_2 = 1$.

Note that the second condition will never be satisfied once the service zone covers the user location. The user facing direction is also considered in locality satisfaction for choosing interaction services that deployed in I/O devices. If the user facing direction is unavailable in the environment, β_2 could be set to zero.

2.5.2.3   QoS Satisfaction

QoS satisfaction is concerned with nonfunctional requirements, which is an important part of user experience. Assume that QoS has N dimensions. Each dimension could be price, availability, latency, and so on. The QoS Satisfaction of service s for a primitive task t is defined as

$$\Psi_Q(t,s) = \frac{1}{N}\sum_{i=1}^{N} \delta_i \times \psi(p_i), \quad \sum_{i=1}^{N}\delta_i = 1 \quad (2.6)$$

where p_i is the ith dimension of QoS, which could be price, availability, latency, and so on. δ_i is the weight coefficient for p_i in QoS; $\psi(p_i)$ is the user satisfaction of the p_i dimension, which can be calculated as

(1) In the case when a smaller value of the p_i dimension indicates a higher degree of user satisfaction (e.g., price), the user satisfaction of the p_i dimension can be computed by

$$\psi(p_i) = \begin{cases} 0 & p_i \geqslant p_{max} \\ \dfrac{p_{max} - p_i}{p_{max} - p_{min}} & p_{min} < p_i < p_{max} \\ 1 & p_i \leqslant p_{min} \end{cases} \quad (2.7)$$

(2) In the case when a smaller value of the p_i dimension indicates a lower degree of user satisfaction (e.g., availability), the user satisfaction of the p_i dimension can be computed by

$$\psi(p_i) = \begin{cases} 1 & p_i \geqslant p_{max} \\ 1 - \dfrac{p_i - p_{min}}{p_{max} - p_{min}} & p_{min} < p_i < p_{max} \\ 0 & p_i \leqslant p_{min} \end{cases} \tag{2.8}$$

where p_{max} and p_{min} are the upper and lower bound of the p_i dimension, which are dependent on users.

In addition, some QoS dimensions may be described by the concept of ontology (such as confidentiality). We cannot use the two formulae described above. In such circumstances, we employ an ontology similarity algorithm to calculate the dimensions of user satisfaction.

2.5.3 Task-to-Service Mapping Algorithm

The framework of task-to-service mapping algorithm is shown in Algorithm 2.1. It takes the TPN as input, and output the best matched services for each primitive task of TPN. Firstly, it selects all the reachable services deployed in the smart environment. "Reachable" means the service zone covers the location of the user. The mapping will be skipped for each primitive task whose status is "*Completed.*" After service filtering and service matching, the service with highest score of satisfaction is chosen.

2.6 TaskShadow: An OSGi-Based Implementation

We implement the proposed scheme and develop an OSGi-based platform for task migration, named TaskShadow, meaning tasks follow a user like his/her shadow. The OSGi is a specification for dynamic java component development and management. Our system is based on the Equinox 3.4 (an open-source OSGi implementation of OSGi R4.1 specification) and J2SE 1.6. The architecture of TaskShadow is shown in Fig. 2.5, which consists of four major modules.

Migration Management (MM) is the core part of our system. It manages the process of task migration, including the trigger of migration, task state management, task-to-service mapping, and event manager. By monitoring associated context acquired from the Context Management, MM determines when a task migration should occur. It uses the event manager to coordinate and control other modules,

---

Algorithm 2.1 Framework of task-to-service mapping algorithm

Input: $TPN \rightarrow$ the Task Petri Net;
Output: $\mathfrak{R} = \{(T_1, S_{k_1})\}, \cdots, \{(T_n, S_{k_n})\} \rightarrow$ the best matched services for TPN;

Generate the set of reachable services $\mathfrak{S}$;
Assign $\emptyset$ to $\mathfrak{R}$;
for each T_i in the primitive task set of TPN
   if status of T_i is *Completed*
      Insert $(T_i, \emptyset)$ into the set and continue;
   end if
   begin Semantic Service Filtering stage
      Functionality Filtering;
      Environment Context Filtering;
      if T_i is *Paused* and has internal state
         Task State Filtering;
      end if
   end Semantic Service Filtering stage
   if $\mathfrak{S}'$ is null
      Insert $(T_i, \emptyset)$ into the set $\mathfrak{R}$ and continue;
   end if
   for each S_j in the filtered set $\mathfrak{S}'$
      begin Service Mapping stage for T_i and S_j
         Calculate the *Locality Satisfaction*;
         Calculate the *Capability Satisfaction*;
         Calculate the *QoS Satisfaction*;
         Calculate the Total Satisfaction;
      end Service Mapping stage
   end for
   Determine the best service S_{k_i} for the primitive task T_i
   Insert (T_i, S_{k_i}) into the set $\mathfrak{R}$;
end for

---

implemented in the message-driven mechanism. The current implementation supports the events of userLeave, userEnter, taskSave, taskRestore, and taskMapping.

Task Management (TM) maintains users' tasks, including TPNs and primitive tasks' description. It can be deployed in user's portable devices. When a primitive task of TPN is activated, TM will send a corresponding task description to MM for task-to-service mapping. When receiving the event of taskSave or taskRestore, TM will save/restore the state of current TPN if the event of taskSave/taskRestore is received.

Service Management (SM) manages the services of a smart environment. The service repository is to store available services' information. If a device comes or leaves, it will register or unregister the services of the device to the service repository. If a task recovery happens, MM will search the service repository for task-to-service mapping. Devices can join in and become services by the adapter

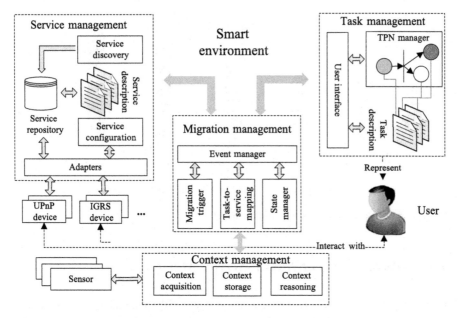

Fig. 2.5   Architecture of TaskShadow platform

layer. The current version of TaskShadow supports uPnP protocol (Universal Plug and Play), which is a core component of the DLNA standard (Digital Living Network Alliance), and IGRS standard (Intelligent Grouping and Resource Sharing) devices.

Context Management (CM) is for collecting and managing context information of a smart environment. It acquires low-level contexts from sensors deployed in the environment and infers high-level context by a rule-based reason engine.

If developers want to build a new task for a user, what they need to do is to create the TPN for the task and give the semantic description of each primitive task associated with the TPN using task ontology. Our TaskShadow provides TPN templates and a primitive task database to avoid starting from scratch. If developers hope to create migration-supported services to join the TaskShadow infrastructure, they should implement two interfaces for each service, stateSave and stateRestore and provide the semantic description of the services based on service ontology.

2.7   Evaluation

We conduct two experiments to evaluate two main features of our system: the performance of task-to-service mapping when varying the service number and the time cost of task migration.

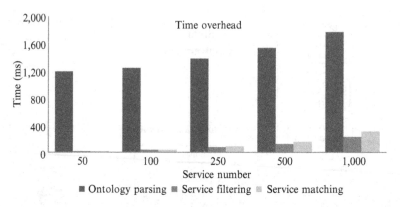

Fig. 2.6 Performance of the task-to-service mapping

2.7.1   Performance of Task-to-Service Mapping

In this experiment, tasks and services are automatically generated to simulate the real world. Each task has 5–15 primitive tasks and each service contains one or two *Capabilities*, one *QoS*, one *ServiceZone*, zero or one *StateInterface*. The description of tasks and services are represented with reference to ontologies. The ontologies used for the experiment contain 66 OWL classes and 31 properties. The hardware for simulation is a laptop computer with 1.60 GHz CPU and 1 Gb memory.

We calculate the time cost for each task-to-service mapping when the service number varies from 50 to 1,000. The result averaged over 20 simulation runs is shown in Fig. 2.6. The time cost is illustrated in three parts, respectively, the time cost for parsing ontology models and related descriptions, the time cost for filtering services by environment context and task state, and the time cost to figure out the best service by matching. We can observe that the time cost of service filtering and service matching is negligible when compared to that of ontology parsing, which is mandatory due to the use of semantic description. Fortunately, the time cost of ontology parsing increases slowly when the service number rises, which is due to the fact that the computation overhead is mainly caused by analysis of ontology models but not by parsing related description. Ontology models are independent of the service number.

2.7.2   Time Cost for Task Migration of "Watch Movie"

The task of "Watch Movie" is taken as the sample to evaluate the time cost of migration from one environment to another. We develop the required services using the TaskShadow platform for "watch movie" and deploy them in two separate

Table 2.1 Average time cost of different stages in the task migration (in ms)

Stages	Average time ($\pm$std.)
Streaming process service	$1,934(\pm73)$
Display service	$2,377(\pm101)$
Speaker service	$2,553(\pm76)$
Migration response time	$3,490(\pm110)$

rooms. The Ubisense localization system is installed to sense the user location. Five volunteers are recruited and are asked to watch the movie, randomly moving from one room to another. Each volunteer repeats the migration ten times.

Table 2.1 shows the result of the average time cost for the streaming process, display service, and speaker service, and the migration response time for the task migration. The "migration response time" means the interval between the beginning of task migration and the time when the user receives video or voice information after the task migration. Note that the time cost shown in the table includes the time overhead of task-to-service mapping. From the table, we learn that the migration response time is about 3.5 s, which is not exactly equal to the sum of the other three stages. It is because the display stage and speaker stage can be processed in parallel.

2.8   Conclusion

This chapter presents a service-based and user-centric solution towards seamless task migration, especially for those tasks involved in local appliances in a smart environment. The underlying assumption of our solution is that a task can be decomposed into a series of primitive tasks. With a semantic model for smart environments and tasks, primitive tasks can be processed separately to search semantically the service space of a smart environment for a best matched service to achieve seamlessness of task migration. The proposed task model and the task-to-service mapping algorithm work effectively to connect user-side tasks and system-side services, so that user tasks can follow users continuously when they move across smart environments.

References

1. Takasugi K, Nakamura M, Tanaka S, Kubota M (2003) Seamless service platform for following a user's movement in a dynamic network environment. In: Titsworth F (ed) The 1st IEEE international conference. Pervasive Computing and Communication (PerCom'03), Texas, IEEE Computer Society Press, pp 71–78
2. Mokhtara SB, Georgantasa N, Issarnya V (2005) Ad hoc composition of user tasks in pervasive computing environments. In: Gschwind T, Assmann U, Nierstrasz O (eds) 4th international workshop on software composition , Edinburgh, UK. Lecture notes in computer science, vol 3628, pp 31–46, Springer, Berlin, Heidelberg

3. Wang ZY, Garlan D (2000) Task-driven computing. Technical report TR CMU-CS-00–154, May, Carnegie Mellon University
4. Pan G, Xu YQ, Wu ZH, Yang L, Lin M, Li SJ (2011) TaskShadow: towards seamless task migration across smart environments. IEEE Intell Syst 26(3):50–57
5. Mokhtara SB, Preuveneersb D, Georgantasa N, Issarnya V, Berbersb Y (2008) EASY: Efficient semAntic Service discoverY in pervasive computing environments with QoS and context support. J Syst Softw 81(5):785–808
6. Román M, Ho H, Campbell RH (2002) Application mobility in active spaces. In: 1st international conference on mobile and ubiquitous multimedia, Oulu, Finland
7. Preuveneers D, Berbers Y (2008) Pervasive services on the move: smart service diffusion on the OSGi framework. In: Sandnes FE, Zhang Y, Rong C, Yang LT, Ma J (eds) 5th international conference on ubiquitous intelligence and computing (UIC'08), Oslo, Norway. Lecture notes in computer science, vol 5061, pp 46–60, Springer, Berlin, Heidelberg
8. Yu P , Cao JN , Wen WD, Lu J (2006) Mobile agent enabled application mobility for pervasive computing. In: 3rd International conference on ubiquitous intelligence and computing (UIC'06), Wuhan, China. Lecture notes in computer science, vol 4159, pp 648–657
9. Zhou Y, Cao JN, Raychoudhury V, Siebert J, Lu J (2007) A middleware support for agent-based application mobility in pervasive environments. In: 5th International workshop on mobile distributed computing (MDC'07), in conjunction with ICDCS'07, Toronto, Canada
10. Satyanarayanan M, Kozuch MA, Helfrich CJ, O'Hallaron DR (2005) Towards seamless mobility on pervasive hardware. Pervasive Mobile Comput 1(2):157–189
11. Xu YQ, Li SJ, Pan G (2009) ScudOSGi: enabling facility-involved task migration in OSGi framework. In: The 4th frontier of computer science and technology (FCST'09), Shanghai, China
12. Murata T (1989) Petri nets: properties analysis and applications. Proc IEEE 77(4):541–580
13. Pérez AG, Corcho O (2002) Ontology specification languages for the semantic web. IEEE Intell Syst 17(1):54–60
14. Liu JS, Issarny V (2004) QoS-aware service location in mobile ad-hoc networks. In: 5th IEEE international conference on mobile data management (MDM'04), Berkeley, CA, pp 224–235
15. Paolucci M, Kawamura T, Payne TR, Sycara K (2002) Semantic matching of web services capabilities. In: Horrocks I, Hendler J (eds) 1st international semantic web conference (ISWC'02), Sardinia, Italia. Lecture notes in computer science, vol 2342, pp 333–347, Springer, Berlin, Heidelberg

Chapter 3
Context-Awareness in SmartShadow

Abstract The capability of context-awareness is indispensable in developing a SmartShadow system. However, there are many challenges to be covered, such as context acquisition, context modeling, context reasoning, and context distribution and utilization. This chapter proposes a new scheme to address these challenges. A three-layer context model is presented to represent various contexts, A context service infrastructure is established to provide large-scale environmental context services toward integration of cyber-physical space. A context-driven rule inference is proposed to make systems adaptive to ever-changing contexts.

3.1 Introduction

With the development of mobile devices and wireless communication technologies, users and devices will face a new environment. With the ability of mobile computing, a distributed embedded system will face an environment full of change, such as devices entering or leaving, the resource being available or unavailable, and the network topology varying with time. The system must know and adapt to these changes. The adaptive ability to handle the environment changes is indispensable in presenting mobile embedded systems, which we call context-awareness. The development of context-awareness computing alleviates computer users from the shackles of desktop computing, and helps users focus on the task itself.

The context comes from the sensors to acquire the state of the environment, the devices and the users, which will be processed into meaningful information to invoke or trigger corresponding services. For context-aware computing, there exist many challenges [1] that need to be covered, such as context acquisition, context modeling, context reasoning, context distribution and utilization. Context acquisition focuses on how to deal with heterogeneous, mass and ambiguous sensor data and gain useful information. Context modeling is for specifying the intrinsic properties and the relationship between contexts. Context distribution use

Z. Wu and G. Pan, *SmartShadow: Models and Methods for Pervasive Computing*, Advanced Topics in Science and Technology in China, DOI 10.1007/978-3-642-36382-5_3, © Zhejiang University Press, Hangzhou and Springer-Verlag Berlin Heidelberg 2013

some subscription/publishing and event triggering mechanisms to distribute context throughout the system. The utilization of context is different in the existing projects. Context can be utilized at a different granularity or level, such as the application level, the device level and the component level.

We propose our context model [2, 3]. This model is composed of three layers, a sensor layer, atom layer, and context layer.

Sensor Data

This is the output of the sensor layer. In current context-aware systems, a great diversity of sensors are used to detect position, touch, motion, voice, gesture, etc.

Context Atom

A context atom is a meaningful assertion retrieved from the sensor data and the assertion cannot be divided into more trivial ones. We use predicate logic to express the assertion such as Person (TOM) and Location (ROOM201).

Context Situation

A certain context situation can be derived from available atoms. A context situation is a trigger point that the system reaches, which represents the current state of the system. Triggering means execution of corresponding services.

In order to simplify the development of context-aware systems and effectively support the establishment of a variety of feature-rich context-aware systems, various types of context-aware middleware are emerging that generally consist of context modeling, storage, reasoning and subscribing-publishing capabilities. Cyber-Physical System (CPS) is a new type of context-aware system, which represents the next generation of computing system development. Making full use of a large number of sensing devices to capture contextual information and supplying environmental context services is the core technology of CPS. However, the existing context service infrastructure rarely considers the relationship to physical space and is limited with respect to system size, service delivery, scalability, etc. We take the cyber-physical space integration systems as application background, examined several challenges with large-scale environmental context services infrastructures, and conducted a number of effective works as following: (1) We proposed a cyber-physical space integrated environmental context model and discussed three aspects of this model from the viewpoint of context space management, device management service management respectively. (2) Based on the model above, we proposed a context services infrastructure for cyber-physical space integration named ScudContext [4]. ScudContext utilizes semantic technology, a spatial-tree model and SOA framework to reflect well the contextual evolution of physical space, supply large-scale environmental context services for cyber-physical integration, and support the advantages of loosely coupled architecture, easy collaboration, scalability and standardized interfaces, etc. (3) We implemented the ScudContext framework in C++ for the Windows platform. Finally, we used a simulation experiment called a sensing-building system to illustrate ScudContext's operating mechanism and show the characteristics of the ScudContext framework.

From the 1980s until now, many projects were developed or are in the progress, such as [4–7], which lay emphasis on the infrastructure of context acquisition, utilization, representation and model of context. However, little emphasis has been laid on context reasoning. Context reasoning enables computing systems to alter adaptively according to the ever-changing contexts so as to provide users services and information for their current tasks more reliably. To do this, developing an effective inference mechanism is critical. Context-aware computing shows new characteristics such as having to be context-driven, to deal with frequent changes in context, to work in a real-time manner and having to program the physical space of the computing locus, which are all different from traditional methods. New characteristics put forward a number of challenges on the reasoning engine. We have analyzed the features of the context-aware computing inference engine distinct from the traditional inference engine. On this basis, we have presented a context-triggered rule-based inference engine ScudCORE [8,9] with its architecture and corresponding mechanisms. We have also realized a prototype of ScudCORE taking the open-source engine CLIPS as the foundation.

3.2 Hierarchical Context Model

We categorize context data into three layers according to the degree of abstraction and semantics: sensor layer, context atom layer, and context situation layer, as shown in Fig. 3.1. The sensor layer is the source of context data, the context atom layer serves as an abstraction between the physical world and semantic world, and the context situation layer provides a description of complex facts with fusion of context atoms.

(1) Sensor data: We use S to denote the output set of the sensor layer.

$$S = S_{t,1}, S_{t,2}, \cdots, S_{t,n}, \ S_{t,i} = (V_t, t, q_i) \tag{3.1}$$

where $S_{t,i}$ denotes the sensor output set of sensor i at time t, V_t is the value of sensor i at time t, and q_i is the degree of credibility of the value.

(2) Context atom: We use A to denote the atom set.

$$A = (A_{t,1}, A_{t,2}, \cdots, A_{t,m}), \ A_{t,i} = (\Gamma_i, t, q) \tag{3.2}$$

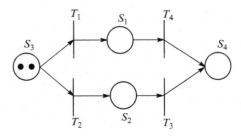

Fig. 3.1 The three-layer context model

where $A_{t,i}$ denotes a semantic piece retrieved from sensor i at time t, called a context atom. Γ denotes an assertion retrieved from the sensor data with the assistance of ontology technology, which cannot be divided into more trivial assertions.

(3) Context situation: We use C to denote the situation set.

$$C = (C_1, \cdots, C_s), \quad C_i = (A_i, \text{Ser}_i, p_i), \quad \text{where } A_t = (A_{t,1}, \cdots, A_{t,i}) \qquad (3.3)$$

A context situation represents the current state of an entity. A_i denotes the set of atoms that constitute a situation. Ser_i denotes the sets of services that should be performed in this situation, which may be null. p_i is the priority of a situation. We define the priority of situations for safety higher than those for entertainment.

3.2.1 Context Atom Layer

A context atom is the information directly available from the physical environment, and this information is relatively simple and basic. Its significance is a basic constitution unit of knowledge representation in the pervasive computing environment. As the context atom is the basic unit, we should guarantee its reusable and shareable characteristics.

The information obtained from various sensors usually consists of electrical signals, magnetic signals, or mathematical value and is not understandable by the high-level systems. Therefore, it is necessary to convert and map these values to understandable context classes, and one context class corresponds to one type of sensor. After the formation of different classes, we should give each class a meaningful semantic tag. W3C Semantic Web Group defines two important standards for developing an ontology: RDF provides descriptions of the data model and OWL provides XML-based syntax to define ontologies. The advantages of using ontology technology is semantic representation and, more importantly, sharing common understanding among different context systems. In addition, multiple ontology libraries can be combined to form a larger ontology library. After the process of semantic representation, sensor data become unified format, meaning-rich context data, and can be directly used by upper-level services and applications.

3.2.2 Context Situation Layer

A context situation refers to a description obtained directly from the physical environment for the current status of a system or environment and is derived from a combination of the context atom, including fusion and reasoning.

A purely static model is not appropriate for the dynamic pervasive computing environment, while a fully dynamic model, which is generated only in runtime, is beyond control and prediction. Therefore, we provide a context situation model based on state and state transition: each context situation is defined as a state node, and the migration between contexts is modeled as transition between states. Because various types of events in the pervasive computing environment can be definitely defined, we are only concerned with those critical points that require systems to respond. For example, when a user enters a car, the system needs to identify the user and determine whether he/she is driving to work according to the time and the schedule. In this example, "a user is driving to work" is a situation that requires a response. The number of situations is limited, so the topology of the context situation model (the number of nodes and relations between nodes) can be pre-defined statistically. At runtime, the transition between each node is measured according to the dynamic occurrence of the current environment. This model guarantees dynamicity, controllability and predictability simultaneously.

Since a Petri-net [10] has powerful ability to describe a parallel event and causation, we employ a Petri-net to model the context network. A Petri-net has two major components called place and transition, corresponding to context situation and migration between contexts of our context network, respectively.

3.2.2.1 Definition of Context Situation State

A place is a logic description of a system state, responding to a context situation. Each context situation is a fusion C of a context atom, where $\sum C = \sum A_1 \times \sum A_2 \times \cdots \times \sum A_m$. Each $\sum A_i$ is a class of context atom. A transition is an event or behavior that occurred, representing the relation between context situations. The formalized definition is as follows:

Definition 3.1. A context network is a five-tuple

$$SN = < S, T, F, W, M_0 > \tag{3.4}$$

where:

$S = \{s_1, s_2, \cdots, s_m\}$: a finite set of states;
$T = \{t_1, t_2, \cdots, t_m\}$: a finite set of transitions;
$F \subseteq (P \times T) \cup (T \times P)$: an arc set of states and transitions;
$W \to \{1, 2, 3, \cdots\}$: a weight function of each transitions;
$M_0 : S \to \{0, 1, 2, 3, \cdots\}$: a function represents the number of tokens for all states at the initial conditions.

Definition 3.2. The state nodes of the model are divided into two categories:

(1) Trigger state node: When a system reaches this state, it must respond to activate the appropriate services. Therefore, the trigger state node is also called crisis state node.
(2) Nontrigger state node: It refers to the node that does not require system response, called critical state node.

Fig. 3.2 Parallel relationship
modeling of
context situations

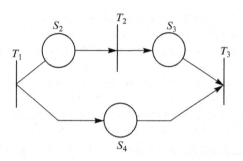

Definition 3.3. The model allows three types of state transition between context situations:

(1) Nontrigger state → trigger state: This transition represents a change from critical state to crisis state, which means a service will be triggered.
(2) Trigger state → nontrigger state: After a specific service is triggered for dealing with the crisis, the system state returns to the critical state. Because the trigger state must return to its critical state, there is no transition between trigger states.
(3) Nontrigger state → nontrigger state: this transition represents migration of system states in different contents.

3.2.2.2   Definition of Relation Between Context Situations

In the process of the definition of context situations, we must pay attention to the inherent relationship between context situations. Context situations are highly relevant, some relationships between them are quite obvious, some are not so it requires a model for describing and analyzing. Firstly, we define the occurring conditions and the results of the transition; secondly, based on the definition of transition in a Petri-net, we divide the relationships between the context situations into four categories: parallel, conflicting, nested, and causal.

Definition 3.4. The enabling of transition: If all input places P_i of a transition T have at least $w(P_i, T)$, this transition is called enabling. The firing of transition: if a transition is enabling, this transition can be fired. After firing, each input place P_i of T reduces $w(P_i, T)$ tokens, and each output places P_j of T add $w(P_i, T)$ tokens.

Definition 3.5. Parallel relationship: If there is no causal relationship between context S_1 and S_2 and they can happen independently, the relationship between S_1 and S_2 is a parallel relationship, denoted by $S_1 \| S_2$.

Modeling with Petri-net, if there are n parallel contexts and they have one onput context, their input context must have n tokens.

As Fig. 3.2 shows, the context S_1 and S_2 have a parallel relationship. S_3 has two tokens represented by black dots in Fig. 3.2. The weights of transition T_1 and T_2 are

Fig. 3.3 Conflicting relationship modeling of context situations

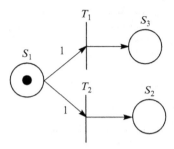

both 1, so T_1 and T_2 can be enabling simultaneously. Context S_1 and S_2 can occur simultaneously, and the order of executing their required services does not matter.

Definition 3.6. Conflicting relationship: If context S_1 and S_2 need to occupy the same resource, such as user attention or device, the relationship between S_1 and S_2 is conflicting, denoted by $S_1 \perp S_2$.

In a conflicting condition, the possible resource competition needs to be addressed. Resource competition includes (1) requests for the same operations from the same resource, for example, requests for an in-car music player to play different music; (2) requests for the opposite operations from the same resource, such as requests for opening or closing a window.

Modeling with Petri-net, if there are n conflicting contexts and they have one output context, their input context can only have 1 token.

As Fig. 3.3 shows, the relationship between context S_1 and S_2 is a conflicting relationship. S_1 only has one token, and the weight of transition T_1 and T_2 are both 1. So, if T_1 is triggered, the number of tokens in S_1 becomes 0, the transition T_2 is not enabling. Otherwise, if T_2 is triggered, then the transition T_1 cannot be triggered. Therefore, it can also mean an "either-or" relationship.

Definition 3.7. Nested relationship: If the context atom set of S_1 is the subset of the context atom set of S_2, the relationship between S_1 and S_2 is a nested relationship, denoted by $S_1 \prec S_2$.

A nested relationship indicates the refinement of knowledge. The corresponding examples include (1) The amount of information increases. For instance, using the user's location, schedule and current time, the current context of the user can be determined as "user is working". However, if we add more information, such as the applications used by the user, the current context of the user can be refined to "user is making work plan table". (2) The accuracy of the context atom increases. For instance, to obtain the user's current location, GPS only detects "user enters a building," but the infrared monitor in the building can detect "user is in room 511." (3) Semantic nesting is brought about by the description information. Description information is the information a user wants to present to different persons. For instance, in an airport, the most important information is "user is Chinese"; and at a business meeting, customers only need to know "user is representative of Zhejiang University." Basically, the nested relationship describes a refinement process based

Fig. 3.4 Nested relationship modeling of context situations

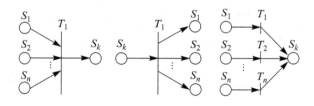

Fig. 3.5 Causal relationship modeling of context situations

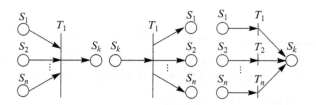

on the increased available information. There is no conflict between nested contexts. Logically, higher refined contexts have more priority, and less refined contexts can be used as background.

Modeling with Petri-net, contexts of different semantic layers are shown in Fig. 3.4. Contexts S_4 and S_2, S_3 belongs to semantic nesting, and S_2, S_3 are the refined process of S_4.

Definition 3.8. Causal relationship: Some context situations are derived from other context situations. This relationship is called a causal relationship, which describes the process of context reasoning.

If S_1 is a precursor of S_2, then:

(1) If S_1 is a nontrigger state, S_2 is a trigger state, or if S_1 is a trigger state, S_2 is a nontrigger state. Then S_2 is only dependent on S_1, called absolute dependence, denoted by $S_1 \mapsto S_2$.
(2) If S_1 and S_2 are both nontrigger states, then S_2 is partially dependent on S_1, denoted by $S_1 \to S_2$.

Modeling with Petri-net, a place represents the context reasoning of an intermediate state in an autonomous system, a transition represents a reasoning process of an autonomous system. If context S_1 and S_2 have a dependent relationship and S_2 is derived from S_1, then there is a transition between S_1 and S_2, and its direction is from S_1 to S_2. In addition, S_1 is the parent node of S_2. A node without any input arrows (it is obtained directly from the sensor) is called a leaf node.

As Fig. 3.5 shows, using Petri-net for modeling the different reasoning relationships as follows:

- IF S_1 and $S_2, \cdots$, and S_n THEN S_k ($CF = u_i$):

$$p_k = \min(p_1 \times u_i, p_2 \times u_i, \cdots, p_n \times u_i) \tag{3.5}$$

- IF S_k THEN S_1 and $S_2, \cdots,$ and S_n $(CF = u_i)$:

$$p_1 = p_2 = \cdots = p_n = p_k \times u_i \tag{3.6}$$

- IF S_1 or $S_2, \cdots,$ or S_n THEN S_k $(CF = u_i)$:

$$p_k = \max\left(p_1 \times u_i, p_2 \times u_i, \cdots, p_n \times u_i\right) \tag{3.7}$$

where p_k is the confidence of context i, CF is the confidence of this rule.

3.3 ScudContext: Large-Scale Environmental Context Services

CPS are new types of pervasive systems, which represent the development direction of the next generation of computing systems. Fully using the context collected by large quantities of sensing devices and supplying environment context services are one of the core technologies of CPS. The existing context infrastructures consider less the relationship between infrastructure and physical space. Also, they are weak on the system scale, service supply mode and system scalability. In this section, we propose a cyber-physical space integrated context model, based on which we propose a cyber-physical space corresponding context management infrastructure "ScudContext". ScudContext utilizes semantic technology, a spatial-tree model and SOA framework, so as to well reflect the evolution of physical space. Moreover, ScudContext can supply large-scale environment context services towards the integration of cyber-physical space, which has some obvious advantages, such as being loosely coupled, with easy collaboration, scalability, standardization of interfaces, etc.

3.3.1 Context Management

The context of physical space covers a wide range, including voice, video, light intensity, temperature, location, etc., with strong heterogeneity. Information services that serve users must meet the user's habits. We need effective data modeling in information processing, because information should be structured as much as possible with user-friendly understanding and organization.

3.3.1.1 Context Management in Cyber-Physical Spaces

With sensing devices available at lower and lower prices, demands on sensing devices are growing significantly. Physical spaces are filled with sensing devices which are causing a continuous information explosion. How to effectively manage

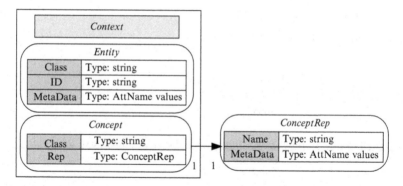

Fig. 3.6 Context modeling for management

large amounts of data becomes a difficulty. Previously, a large amount of studies on a centralized approach were made [5], which become most suitable for effective information management in a small-scale physical environment, such as smart homes [11] or smart offices [12]. However, for large-scale information acquisition and management, we need a distributed framework for effective organization of information.

3.3.1.2   Model of Context Management

Description of Context, Context Space, and Service

In reference [5], it is suggested that the context is the characterization of an entity's status; an entity can be a person, place, or objects related to the user and system. Starting from the description of the context, the context must be associated with a particular entity and entity status information with entities form a context. As a combination of these ideas, we propose our context management model shown in Fig. 3.6. For any context, it consists of an entity and an information called Concept, each of which has one or more representations called ConceptRep. Meta-information related to Entity and ConceptRep is represented as key-value pairs called MetaData. For example, if room temperature is a Context, then the room is an Entity, the temperature is a Concept.

Based on our model, we have established context ontology instances for large-scale environments. With ontology description, entities in a physical environment can be classified, and ontology can also unify the expression of the concept, to a unified semantic representation of context. Figure 3.7 shows the construction of a context model. Drawing on the idea to separate representation and concepts in the literature [3, 7], a Concept can be expressed in a variety of ways as ConceptRep. Different representations can be defined between the transforming relationships. Thus the Location is a Concept, which can be represented in the GPS, and can also be represented in a geographical location.

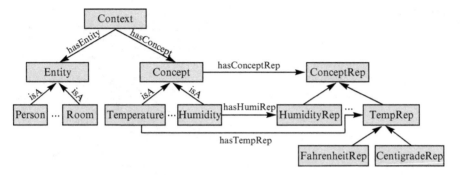

Fig. 3.7 Construction of context model

Sensing devices can sense physical space environmental data. After processing, such data forms structural context information consistent with the habits of users. This is a mapping procedure from physical space to context space. A context space corresponds to a physical space, managing entities, context sources (here, context sensing devices) in the physical space, and provides users with context information services. Entities are the basic units of context space management, because they are the physical basis of the context and a context is always associated with an entity. With entities, a group context associated with the entity can be managed. Context space, as a large-scale infrastructure in the physical environment, is responsible for collecting, processing context, and for providing context services.

Organization of Context Space and Service

Context service requires effective management of many heterogeneous devices in large spaces. As increasingly complex application system makes a very high demands on upper service delay, scalability, and flexibility. The current commonly used context services are centralized schemes, in which context storage, management and distribution are concentrated in one or several centers servers. By this way it is difficult to meet the requirements of efficiency of management. Due to the close relationship between the required context of an application system and local physical spaces, we divide and organize the entire context service into composed services located in subspaces with different levels and grain size. Such subspaces correspond to a physical spaces and can provide a context service in different grains according to the requirements of the application systems. Subspaces have a hierarchical relationship and these levels reflect different resolutions and the containment relationship between subspaces.

With the above ideas, the physical space is mapped into a hierarchical tree structure in the context of space, as shown in Fig. 3.8. Each node of the space tree corresponds to a context space. Device management, access and extension in physical spaces are mapped to management, access and expansion in subspaces and context services at all levels.

Fig. 3.8 Illustration of
context space tree

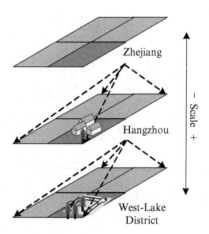

The top of the space tree is a node called the Top Context Space (TCS), which is the unity entry of all the context spaces and the abstract of the entire physical space. TCS space maintains the structure of the space tree, keeping basic information, including the space name, host address, entities and other information, as well as the space containing service information for each context space. For registration, cancellation of subspaces, you will need to apply first to TCS. After success, TCS will make the appropriate adjustments to the structure of the space tree. Subspaces in different levels with similar structures and functions, the main function of which is to manage their corresponding physical space sensing devices and provides context service for the query and management, and to maintain information such as name, location, coverage, manager, etc., related to this space and its underlying subspaces. Subspace can have lower subspaces. A lower subspace must be located in the physical space corresponding to its subspace in its parent space, such as a room space in a building space. With this tiered approach mapping context space to the physical spaces of different size, you can more efficiently organize and manage context and make it easier for the support needs for different granularities of the context service.

When building a new context-aware infrastructure (including sensing, communications, computing devices, etc.) in a physical space, you can create a new subspace as an extension of the original context space tree. When a subspace is created, it first builds descriptions of its own basic information. Then it can run as a separate space, receiving device registrations to provide local context services. But it is isolated, can only react to local system calls, until it is registered as a space in the existing space in a space tree, and can be used as part of the tree. After linking up with other spaces, they collaborate to provide context services.

When a new space node applies to register into a TCS, TCS will examine the authenticity and rationality information of the new space, to guarantee the context space will contain the corresponding relationship between physical spaces. After review, TCS will assist the new space to link to an existing space as parent, and update the space tree structure of TCS. With new spaces created and joined, and the exit of old spaces, the space tree TCS keeps evolving, but always maintains the mapping of physical spaces.

Context spaces organize and deliver related functions in related physical spaces, such as space registration, cancellation and context query, subscription and even more complex services for applications. Users and applications who request services need to locate the target space through the TCS, and gather a description of services, before accessing a specific service.

3.3.2 The ScudContext Infrastructure

Based on our context management model, we propose an infrastructure for context management in Cyber-Physical Space, which is named ScudContext. ScudContext takes a context space as a unit, manages context sources like sensors within a physical space, and provides context service. It describes context in semantic descriptions, to enable context sharing and service collaboration in complicated applications; it encapsulates context sources into services with service protocol stacks such as DPWS, and enables context service management in SOA, which makes the system loosely coupled with easy collaboration and standardized service interface.

3.3.2.1 Overview

As shown in Fig. 3.9, the infrastructure of ScudContext consists of four layers, each of which is responsible for a special function.

The bottom is the context source layer. Context sources are encapsulated as services and uploaded and registered into the context space with unified management. A service can either join a space during space initialization or be dynamically discovered and plugged-in by a running space. After registration, context information produced by the context source is shared in the whole space tree.

The second layer is called the basic function layer, with three main components:

(1) Context Source Management, which manages context sources in the space and provides registration and cancellation services.
(2) Data Management, which manages raw data gathered by context sources, and provides query and subscription services for context.
(3) Space Management, which maintains descriptions related to context spaces and provides management services for space tree, such as registration and cancellation of services.

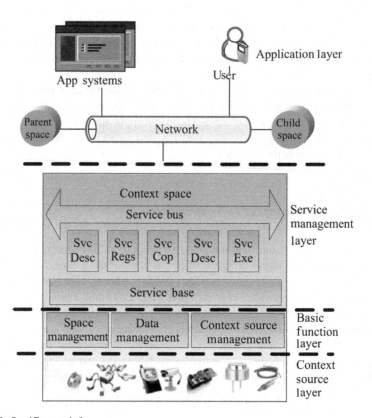

Fig. 3.9 ScudContext infrastructure

The third layer is service management layer, which manages all services in a context space. In this layer, there is a service description store with semantic descriptions and interface descriptions of all services in this space. In addition, it provides common functions of SOA, such as service registration, service discovery, service composition, and service execution.

The top layer is an application layer, in which context-aware systems, mobile users, and other entities in space interact with context spaces through services, in order to accomplish certain tasks.

3.3.2.2 Context Service Management

Recently, SOA has attracted a wide range of industrial and academic attention due to its uniformed service encapsulation and standardized interaction interfaces that can realize loosely coupled service management and cooperation between heterogeneous platforms.

We adopt SOA to integrate our systems. Functions provided by a context space are encapsulated into services via WSDL(Web Service Description Language),

UDDI(Universal Description Discovery and Integration), SOAP(Simple Object Access Protocol), and other standardized protocols in SOA.

There are two types of services provided by a context space, namely, basic service and extended service. Basic services are those directly related to context spaces, like registration, cancellation, deployment, query and subscription of context sources. Extended services are those services composed of basic services or those services processing information gathered by context sources. For service consumers, the two types of services are transparent. Context service management is as follows:

(1) A service is described in WSDL
(2) The service is registered to TCS via UDDI specification.
(3) A service consumer can access TCS via UDDI interface to get service location and descriptions.
(4) The consumer can access the service via SOAP.
(5) The service is executed and results returned.

3.3.2.3 Context Space Creation, Registration and Cancellation

There are two main steps in the creation of a context space, space information generation, and space initialization. Space information contains the space name, location, coverage range, and manager of information. Space initialization includes initialization of entities, context sources, service interfaces, etc. The procedure for space registration is shown in Fig. 3.10.

3.3.2.4 Query and Subscription Algorithms for Context Space

Query and subscription are most fundamental and commonly used context services. Query is a synchronized process, in which service consumers send request to context space and wait for the result returned from services. Subscription is a asynchronous process. Service consumers send a request but do not wait; the space will send the result back a moment later.

Consumers of query and subscription can be either application systems or mobile users. Considering different application requirements and the features of ScudContext frameworks, we propose three modes of query and subscription. Taking query service as an example, there are three types of query services: entity-oriented query, space-oriented query, and subspace-based integrated query. Each kind of query has a similar execution process, with the following steps, but each is handled differently.

(1) Generate a query request and encapsulates the request in a SOAP envelope.
(2) If a consumer knows the physical location or network address of a context service, his request is sent directly to the required space, otherwise the request is sent to the TCS space, which locates the service space with the space tree and redirects the request to it.
(3) The required service executes the request and returns a result.

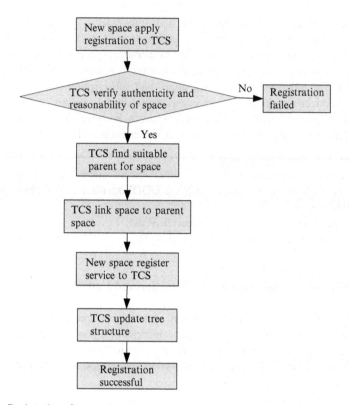

Fig. 3.10 Registration of context space

Entity-Oriented Query

An entity-oriented query is used to query specific information of a certain entity (or a type of entities), noted as $Query(space, entity\_id | entity_class[concept])$, including four query patterns. In the query, *space* represents the name of the required space; *entity_id* identifies a queried entity; *entity_class* represents use of a class description to query a class of entities; *concept* means the consumer wants to know exactly such concepts of an entity. If omitted, all kinds of context are returned.

Space-Oriented Query

As our context service management framework reflects the mapping between physical spaces and information spaces, it is especially convenient to provide a query interface oriented to physical spaces. We propose two query patterns for spaces, in which a query request places context services in specific spaces and attains specific context information in the space. The query is noted as

Query(*space*[*concept_type*]) in which *space* represents the name of the queried space; *concept_type* is optional, which represents specific classes of context the consumer is concerned with.

SubSpace-Based Integration Query

Sometimes, context information required by an application system cannot be obtained through context services within a specific context space. Instead, the information can be obtained by integrating context information from its subspaces. For example, an application system queries the number of currently working computers in Building A, but obviously it is not provided with a context of "Building A" node in the space tree. However, it is possible to sum working computer numbers of all subspaces (rooms) of Building A to get the total number. ScudContext framework provides the integration query, which places services in different subspaces. Currently supported operations are sum, average number, maximum, minimum. In execution, the request for integration query is dispatched from the required space to its subspaces recursively with the integrated result returned to the user. Integrated query is noted as *Query*(*space*, *context*, *Aggregation*), in which *space* represents the name of the queried space, *context* represents a specific context type, and *Aggregation* represents the integration operation.

3.4 ScudCORE: Context-Driven Reasoning Engine

Pervasive computing puts forward a number of challenges for the reasoning engine, such as the needs to be context-driven, to deal with frequently changing of contexts, and to work in a real-time manner. Traditional reasoning engines can hardly meet these new requirements. In this section, we present a context-driven reasoning engine ScudCORE (Scud COntext-driven Reasoning Engine), which takes the first-order predicate logic as the basis. When contexts vary frequently, ScudCORE reduces the reasoning problems of excessive frequency and inefficiency by the context filtering mechanism. We employ ontology to make the reasoning engine convenient to share, reuse and understand context information both inside and outside of it. Also, we increase its flexibility with a dynamic rule management module.

3.4.1 Context-Driven Reasoning in Pervasive Computing

Compared with traditional reasoning, context-driven reasoning in pervasive computing environments has unique features and requirements in the following way:

(1) Context-driven: Reasoning tasks need to be triggered by context actively. When context information meets particular requirements for services, reasoning starts. Then computation devices are driven by serve users; but traditional reasoners are problem-driven or application-driven.

(2) Frequently context changing: In pervasive computing, there is rich context information that frequently changes with time and space. Traditional reasoning engines are not effective enough to deal with ever-changing contexts.

(3) Real time: In order to serve the user transparently and actively and to assist users' work and life, a reasoning engine needs to work in a real-time manner to serve the user in time.

(4) Open: Facts and rules in pervasive computing are highly dynamic. For different applications and situations, rules might need to be modified to adapt to a new environment.

Therefore, there is an urgent need for a novel context-driven reasoning engine to support pervasive computing applications. With first-order predicate logic and an open expert system toolkit CLIPS [13] as the basis, we provide a context-driven reasoning engine called ScudCORE (ScudCOntext-driven Reasoning Engine). ScudCORE solves problems of over-computation, inefficiency and other problems caused by frequently changing contexts. ScudCORE also introduces a novel context filtering mechanism to promote reasoning efficiency.

3.4.2   ScudCORE Architecture

Based on analysis of traditional reasoning engine functionalities and features of context-aware reasoning, we introduce ScudCORE, which adopts a context filter to lower problems caused by the frequently changing context. It also supports sharing, reusing and understanding of context information with ontology modeling. In addition, with a rule management module, openness and agility of the reasoning engine is enhanced.

The architecture of the ScudCORE reasoning engine is shown in Fig. 3.11. ScudCORE consists of Reasoning Module, Knowledge Base, Rule Base, Rule Monitor, Context Driver, Local Context Base and Executor, in which Reasoning Module, Knowledge Base, and Executor are similar to traditional reasoning engines, and Rule Monitor, Context Driver, and Local Context Base are specially designed for context-driven reasoning in pervasive computing. Functions of each module are listed as following:

(1) Knowledge Base and Rule Base: In Knowledge Base, some facts of expert knowledge in different domains and some common sense facts are stored, which are almost static; In Rule Base, a certain rule set used to reason about user desires is stored.

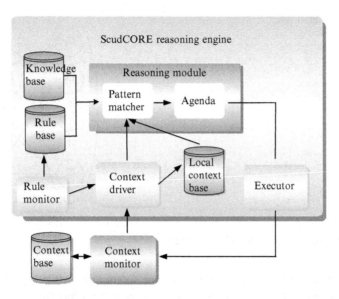

Fig. 3.11 ScudCORE architecture

(2) Reasoning Module: Reasoning Module consists of Pattern Matcher and Agenda. Pattern Matcher takes Knowledge Base, Rule Base, and Local Context Base as inputs to check which rules are met by current facts. Agenda assigns priorities to such rules.

(3) Executor: Executor selects and executes a rule with highest priority and transfers execution results to the outer Context Monitor.

(4) Rule Monitor: Rule Monitor provides addition, deletion, and modification interfaces for rules and examines possible conflicts after a modification of Rule Base. After modification it notifies Context Driver.

(5) Context Driver: Context Driver enables ScudCORE to be a context-driven system. It provides novel approaches to manage context information which solves problems such as frequent context changes and promotes efficiency and agility of the reasoning engine.

(6) Local Context Base: For efficient access and easy management of dynamic context "facts", we put such context information into an independent database in Local Context Base instead of putting it into Knowledge Base.

(7) Context Monitor and Context Base: These two modules are outside ScudCORE, but they directly relate to the context-aware system and ScudCORE engine. Context Monitor provides two functions for ScudCORE. One is to provide needed context information for Context Driver, the other is to update Context Base or trigger an event according to reasoning results and drive computing devices to serve users. Context Base stores all context information about environments.

Fig. 3.12 A context-rule
associated table

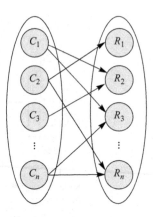

3.4.3   Context-Driven Mechanism

To establish an effective context-driven mechanism for meeting the special needs of
context reasoning, the main strategy adopted includes following two issues:

(1) Context filtering: The pervasive computing environment has rich context infor-
    mation and this information varies frequently. Therefore, in order to accelerate
    the speed of reasoning and build a real-time reasoning system, we add context
    drive to ScudCORE to achieve the purpose of filtering a large amount of context
    information.
(2) Dynamic rule management: According to the requirements of the current
    environment, the context reasoning engine can dynamically add or delete rules
    to greatly enhance the flexibility and capabilities of context reasoning.

We adjust the expert system development tool CLIPS [13] according to the new
architecture and build a new context-driven reasoning engine ScudCORE. Next, we
will detail the context-driven mechanism of ScudCORE.

3.4.3.1   Context Filtering Mechanism

Rule Association – Based Context Filtering

Context collection provides various context information, but not all of the information is required by the context reasoning system. We only need to focus on
the information related to the rules, which can greatly reduce the burden of the
reasoning engine and improve reasoning speed.

Therefore, we maintain a context-rule associated table, as shown in Fig. 3.12,
where C represents context information and R represents rules. The relationships
between context and rules are many, namely, a context can be used in multiple
rules and a rule can also use many different contexts. Through the table, we can
dynamically access a set of contexts which may be used in all rules.

Fig. 3.13 Data structure of context-rule associated table

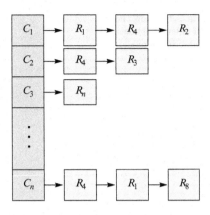

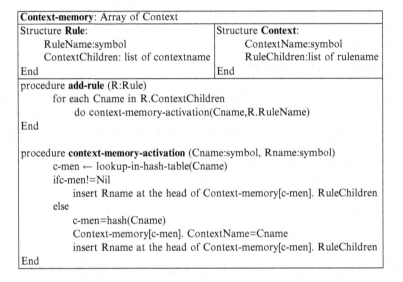

Context-memory: Array of Context	

Structure **Rule**:
    RuleName:symbol
    ContextChildren: list of contextname
End
	Structure **Context**:
	    ContextName:symbol
	    RuleChildren:list of rulename
	End

procedure **add-rule** (R:Rule)
        for each Cname in R.ContextChildren
                do context-memory-activation(Cname,R.RuleName)
End	

procedure **context-memory-activation** (Cname:symbol, Rname:symbol)
        c-men ← lookup-in-hash-table(Cname)
        ifc-men!=Nil
            insert Rname at the head of Context-memory[c-men]. RuleChildren
        else
            c-men=hash(Cname)
            Context-memory[c-men]. ContextName=Cname
            insert Rname at the head of Context-memory[c-men]. RuleChildren
End	

Fig. 3.14 Pseudo codes for context-rule associated table updating: adding a new rule

We use the array to store the name of contexts, as shown in Fig. 3.13. Each context has a unique key, so using a hash table can quickly access the required context. We use a linked list to store the rule set related to a context. When adding a new rule, according to the contexts used in the rule, we add a node of this rule to each linked list of related contexts. If a context used in the rule does not exist, we add the context to the array and then add the new rule node. When deleting a rule, if the linked list of a context is empty, we will remove this context from the array.

Figure 3.14 shows the pseudo-code for how to maintain a context-rule associated table when adding a new rule.

Fig. 3.15 Flow chart
of differential context
subscription model

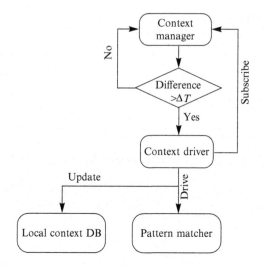

Subscription-Based Context Filtering

Using a context-rule associated table, we can selectively subscribe to the context
manager for required contexts. In the pervasive computing environment, the service
is triggered by the changes in the current contexts. Therefore, only when the contexts
concerned by the context driver have changed, does the context manager send these
contexts to the context driver. It effectively reduces the load on the reasoning engine
when processing a large number of contexts.

However, some contexts are changing continuously, such as temperature, user
location, intensity, speed, etc., so the amount of information the reasoning engine
needs to handle is still very large using the mechanism described above. Here, we
introduce a difference ΔT to improve the previous subscription mechanism. Only
when the difference between the value of a new context T_1 collected by sensors and
the value of current context T_0 stored in the local context database is more than ΔT
does the context manager send the new context to the context driver and update the
local context database using the value of context T_1 simultaneously. It demands the
context manager support the differential context subscription model, which is shown
in Fig. 3.15.

3.4.3.2   Dynamic Rule Management

A context-aware system must provide active service for users at anytime, which
requires that the reasoning engine is running continuously, and our pervasive computing scenarios cannot be static, which often add or remove computing devices.
Then the existing rules of the reasoning engine may not meet new requirements, so
we need to modify the existing rules. If we close the reasoning engine to modify

---

Algorithm 3.1 The framework of rule update algorithm

Detection of rule conflict;
IF there is no conflict, **THEN**
      update the rule database;
      update the Rete matching network;
      update the context-rule associated table;
      modify the subscribed information;
ELSE
      use rules conflict elimination strategy;
      IF there exist new rules needed to update, **THEN**
            CALL rule update;

---

rules and re-start the reasoning engine, the whole system will be entirely paralysed during this time. Therefore, we add a rule management module to ScudCORE, providing the functionality of dynamically adding, deleting, modifying the rules and making the reasoning engine more flexible.

We employ the Rete [14] algorithm to implement the pattern matching algorithm of ScudCORE. The Rete algorithm, as a classic pattern matching algorithm, not only resolves the quick match problem for facts and rules (an improved Rete algorithm can make a large scale context reasoning system support hundreds of thousands of rules run quickly [15]) but also provides a good support to implement the functionality of runtime by dynamically adding, deleting, modifying rules without affecting the running of the whole reasoning engine.

When a rule is updated, we first detect whether the updated rule conflicts with existing rules in the rule database. If there is no conflict, the rule manager will update the rule database and also notify the context driver to update the context-rule associated table for consistency. If there exists a conflict, our current rule manager uses a rule conflict elimination strategy expert system to address this issue [13]. Our rule update algorithm, including rule adding, deleting, and modification, is shown in Algorithm 3.1.

3.5 Conclusion

The capability of context-awareness is indispensable in developing a SmartShadow system. There are many challenges, such as context acquisition, context modeling, context reasoning, and context distribution and utilization. This chapter proposes a new scheme to address these challenges. A three-layer context model is presented to represent various contexts, A context service infrastructure is established to provide large-scale environmental context services towards integration of cyber-physical space. A context-driven rule inference is proposed to make systems adaptive to ever-changing contexts.

References

1. Dey AK, Abowd GD (1999) Towards a better understanding of context and context-awareness. In: Gellersen H-W (ed) Proceedings of the 1st international symposium on Handheld and Ubiquitous Computing. Springer, Heidelberg, pp 304–307
2. Sun J, Wu ZH, Pan G (2009) Context-aware smart car: from model to prototype. J Zhejiang Univ A 10(7):1049–1059
3. Sun J (2009) Research on context model and middleware in smart car. PhD thesis, Zhejiang University (in Chinese)
4. Pan G, Li SJ, Chen YX (2011) ScudContext: large-scale environmental context services infrastructure towards cyber-physical space integration. J Zhejiang Univ (Eng Sci) 45(6):991–998
5. Dey AK (2000) The context toolkit: aiding the development of context-aware applications. In: Ghezzi C, Jazayeri M, Wolf AL (eds) Workshop on software engineering for wearable and pervasive computing, ACM, pp 434–441
6. Ranganathan A, Campbell RH (2003) An infrastructure for context-awareness based on first order logic. Pers Ubiquitous Comput 7(6):353–364
7. Biegel G, Cahill V (2004) A framework for developing mobile, context-aware applications. In: Werner B (ed) Second IEEE international conference on pervasive computing and communications, IEEE Press, pp 361–365
8. Pan G, Li T, Ren HY, Li SJ, Yao M (2009) ScudCORE: a context-driven reasoning engine. Acta Electron Sin 37(S):70–74 (in Chinese)
9. Li T (2009) Context-driven reasoning engine. Master thesis. Zhejiang University (in Chinese)
10. Bonacina MP (1987) Petri nets for knowledge representation. Petri Net Newsl 27:28–36
11. Ma T, et al (2005) Context-aware implementation based on CBR for smart home. In: IEEE international conference on wireless and mobile computing, networking and communications, IEEE Press, pp 112–115
12. Coronato A, De Pietro G, Esposito M (2006) A semantic context service for smart offices. Int Conf Hybrid Inf Technol 2:391–399
13. Giarratano JC, Tiley GD (2005) Expert systems: principles and programming, 4th edn. Thomson, Boston
14. Forgy C (1982) Rete: a fast algorithm for the many pattern/many object pattern match problem. Bobrow DG (ed) Elsevier. Artif Intell 19(1):17–37
15. Doorenbos RB (1993) Matching 100,000 learned rules. In Fikes R, Lehnert WG (eds) Proceedings of the 11th national conference on artificial intelligence (AAAI), MIT Press, pp 290–296

Chapter 4
File Modeling in SmartShadow

Abstract Files are fundamental for information storage in a computing system. This chapter explores the user and environment context to improve personal file management. We focus on the user-oriented files in a computer operating system, which are usually operated manually, such as document files, images, and video files. We formalize the dynamics of contexts to sequential signals, called context streams. Each context stream is a one-dimensional function of time. With the model of a context stream, files can be reorganized using a set of discretely sampled streams based on file operation such as file creating, editing, and deleting. We propose and implement a file system with context streams, named ScudFile. We introduce three applications of the ScudFile, file browsing, file searching, and file recommendation, are introduced. The evaluation of time and usability demonstrates the effectiveness of the ScudFile system.

4.1 Introduction

Files are very important units for storing data in computer operating systems. However, the increasing number of personal files makes them difficult for users to manage and access. In the past few years, the storage capacity of hard disks has increased rapidly. People now do not worry about where to save the data any more. Nevertheless, the challenge that is arising is how can we manage millions of personal files in a convenient manner?

Nowadays, the mainstream operating systems, such as Windows, Linux, and MacOS, basically use a directory, a tree structure, to organize and manage files. In this way, each file has a unique file path and the user can use this path to access a file. The advantage is that a user can create a semantic file path to help find files, for example, we can create a directory of "publication" in the OS and put all the published papers in this directory. But with the growing number of files, the tree directory has exposed many shortcomings.

Z. Wu and G. Pan, *SmartShadow: Models and Methods for Pervasive Computing*, Advanced Topics in Science and Technology in China, DOI 10.1007/978-3-642-36382-5_4, © Zhejiang University Press, Hangzhou and Springer-Verlag Berlin Heidelberg 2013

(1) File classification: To create a semantic file path, users have to classify a file into a category, such as "music", "movie". However, in practice, so many files are difficult to classify in a specific category. They are often suitable for a variety of categories.

(2) Access depth: The more detailed the classification, the deeper the file is stored in the tree directory structure, such as "F:/Music/Ch/Male/Pop/2000/fly.mp3". Users have to go deep into five subdirectories to access the file of "fly.mp3". It is inconvenient for users to access a file with so long a path.

(3) Locating files: Users have to manually specify a path to locate files. However, it is a huge burden for users to remember hundreds of thousands of files. It also causes a huge burden for users to give each directory a meaningful name.

Many efforts have been made to tackle these problems. A virtual file directory is a major solution, which uses various information to describe files and then creates a similar directory access mechanism according to the description. Thus, a user can use the traditional file access method to access files which they want, but the file path is made from the file's description information. Context file system and the semantic file system are examples of a virtual file directory. The context file system uses the context information to describe files, and semantic file system uses semantic information [1, 2]. They both facilitate the work of file search, but they do not alleviate the burden of file management. For either context or semantics as description information, users need to participate in creating a description.

In this chapter, we propose a context organization model [1, 2]–context stream to organize context information for files. It helps users find files quickly by automated description and analysis information. We focus on the files which users will access directly. That means system files are not under our consideration. We divide the files into two categories: user-oriented files and system-oriented files. User-oriented files are those users will operate manually, such as documents, audio, images, and video. System-oriented files are those an operating system needs and users usually do not need to know about, such as temporary files and binary program files. We focus on the user-oriented files.

4.2 Related Work

Nowadays, a file system is one of the basic modules in an operating system. Files are one of the most important storage forms [3]. In an ordinary PC, the number of files almost reaches millions. The growing number of files makes it difficult for users to manage and access them. How to manage users' files? How to find the needed file quickly? These become very important questions.

These semantic file system [4] uses the keywords and property information to describe files and directories. Based on the information, the file system creates a virtual file directory to help users find the files they want. To access a file, the file path will be parsed and translated to attribute-based queries. For example, "User:Tony/Type:PPT/Name:lecture/" will be translated to the queries of "Query(User=Tony) and Query(Type=PPT), Query(Name=lecture)" [4]. This approach makes the sequence of attributes insignificant. The semantic file system has the potential to improve a file search, but the process of description increases the users' burden. Traditionally, semantic information comes from two sources: content analysis and manual configuration. Most users are unwilling to perform the tedious and time-consuming job. In addition, the manual job will bring unpredictable errors. Content analysis obtained the semantic information by analyzing the file path and keywords of file content. The disadvantage of this approach is that the information obtained from content analysis is often misunderstood by users. Even users are sometimes confused by what is the correct value.

A context file system [5, 6] uses the context such as time and location as description information and uses a virtual file directory to access files. The ParcTab [7] project is to integrate context with file access. ParcTab associates files with location information. When users move between different locations, the file browser will change the file list. However, the ParcTab only uses location information to associate files. It has no effect on the files which are not sensitive to locations. The context file system in the Gaia [4, 8, 9] project uses various context information to associate files. In the file system, users associate files and directories with scenarios, which are the combination of context information. When a user enters a pervasive computing environment, the context information from physical devices is compared with the description information of scenarios for preparing the eligible files and directory. Gaia uses context to organize information so that it is easier for users to find desirable material for launched or long-running applications. But it needs users to decide when the files will be used and be manually added, to describe the file. OmniStore [10, 11] is a file system that automatically associates the context information to files. OmniStore needs the support of physical devices to collect all the available context information. When a file is created, OmniStore uses the collected context information to describe the file. It collects context information at regular intervals. In the whole process, users have no burden and can find the files in the context of file creation.

The Google file system (GFS) [3] is a scalable distributed file system for large distributed data. It provides fault tolerance while running on inexpensive hardware. And it delivers high aggregate performance to a large number of clients. There are many products and technologies of Google based on GFS, such as Google Search and Google Mail. GFS adopts one single master node which maintains all file system metadata and multiple chunkservers in one cluster. The client application implements the file system API and communicates with the master and chunkservers to write or read data.

Connections [12] is a file system search tool that provides fast file search. It combines traditional content-based search with context information gathered from user activity. Connections identify temporal relationships between files by tracing file system call and use the relationships to expand and reorder traditional content search results. This is similar to the data pre-fetching of the operating system, which uses the relevance of files to accelerate searching.

4.3 Modeling Files with Context Streams

4.3.1 Context Stream: Dynamics of Contexts

Different from the traditional computing systems, ubiquitous computing systems use context information to allow applications to adapt to a user's environment [13–15]. In order to organize and analyze the context information associated with files better, we propose a context organization model, called Context stream, in which each dynamic context has a context stream. The ith context stream is defined by a continuous sequential signal as a function of time.

$$\mathfrak{C}_i = c_i(t) \tag{4.1}$$

This concept is similar to character stream, audio stream, and video stream. The discrete data, arranged in a certain way, forms a continuous stream of a data set. Time is a special kind of context. Many contexts are dependent on it. Thus we use time as the marking of information organization. For example, the location context stream of a person can be denoted with C_L:

$$C_L = c_{L_1} c_{L_2} c_{L_3} c_{L_4} \cdots \tag{4.2}$$

Figure 4.1 illustrates an example of the location context stream. It shows the changes in location of a person in a day.

Usually we only need to analyze a part of the context information in some discrete samples of the context stream. Here we define the concept of Context Substream. The substream of the ith context is defined as follows, which is a discrete signal sampled from a continuous context stream:

$$A_1 = \{c_1(t_j^1)\}_{j=1}^{N_1} \tag{4.3}$$

It is a subset of a context stream. For example, in the context stream of location, we may only focus on the locations where a user has made file operations.

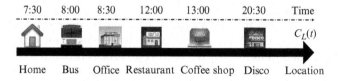

Fig. 4.1 Illustration of the location context stream

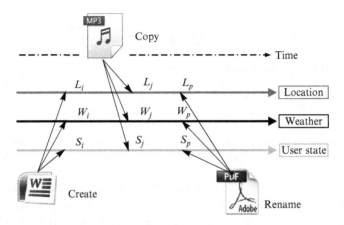

Fig. 4.2 Attaching files onto context streams at points of file operations. Here we show three context streams: location, weather, and user state

4.3.2   Modeling Files with Context Stream

Two aspects are involved when integrating context information with files: (1) When is a file connected with context? (2) Which context information is used to describe files? In order to implement file description automatically, we choose the file operation as the trigger for updating the file description and use the context of the operation as description information.

We hope to use context stream to automatically describe files. The different categories of description information develop different modes of file description. If the context information from the job the file belongs to, is used as the description, users often have to manually specify the job a file is associated with, e.g., the Gaia context file system [9]. Because nobody else knows exactly what the files are for, it is hard to get the context automatically. A semantic file system uses the semantic information as the description which is from directory analysis and content analysis. We choose file operation as the trigger to associate the file with context information, which makes the process of labeling files automatic and temporal. A file operation can be detected by the application from the file system. Compared with the tedious file path, the context of file operation may be easier for users to remember.

As shown in Fig. 4.2, when a file operation happens, the target file will be "hung" on the context stream. Because the environment where users stay contains many kinds of context information, such as location, weather, and user state, the file will be described by multiple context informations. From the perspective of context stream, the target file is hung on multiple context streams. The PDF file in Fig. 4.2 is operated at the time of p. It is hung on the context streams of location, weather, and user state at the point of time p simultaneously.

From Fig. 4.2, we can see that the context stream can be considered as a collection of the points hung with files and without association with any file. The

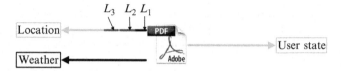

Fig. 4.3 Illustration of context substreams of a single file

points hung with files form a context substream. The time point i, j, and p on the location context stream, arranged in the temporal order, can make up of a context substream, where the file operations happen.

Each single file s is attached by several context substreams, in which we recoded all operations of the target file. As shown in Fig. 4.3, each substream for a specific context contains the file operation history, i.e., showing the file has been operated at which location, in what weather, in what user state, and when.

$$\text{des}(t) = \begin{cases} C_L(t) \\ C_S(t) \\ C_W(t) \end{cases} \tag{4.4}$$

4.4   ScudFile: A Meta File System with Context Streams

In the current operation systems, users locate files in two ways: (1) locate files by browsing in the tree structure "folder/directory"; (2) search files by keywords. However, both methods are inefficient when the amount of files becomes large. We consider a context-aware solution to associate files with context information such as time and location and then use this information to help users to manage the files. In this section, we first describe ScudFile, a file system with context stream, then its implementation. ScudFile is able to associate context stream with files automatically by tracing system calls when users operate on the files. The context streams are used to organize appropriate files for user applications.

4.4.1   Architecture of the ScudFile

Figure 4.4 illustrates the architecture of ScudFile. It builds upon traditional file systems such as NTFS, FAT32, and EXT2. From a user's perspective, ScudFile is a kind of file manager like Total Commander. Internally, ScudFile traces user's file operations and automatically associates files with context streams, and then helps with file management. Its architecture is composed of five modules: Tracer, Context Acquisition, Context Description, Context Analysis, and Context Management.

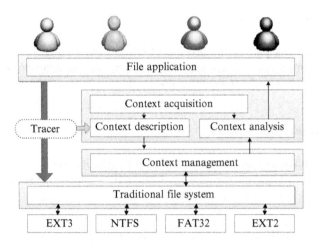

Fig. 4.4 ScudFile architecture

4.4.1.1   Tracer

This module sits between the file application and the file system, monitoring the file operations. Because our system focuses on the file operations only from users, but not from the system, Tracer needs to distinguish the user-oriented files and the system-oriented files. Tracer is the trigger point when the ScudFile starts to update context streams of files.

4.4.1.2   Context Acquisition

This module is responsible for getting context information. In our system, we describe the file with context information at each point of the file operation. This module needs to provide context information in a nearly real-time manner since outdated information will affect the accuracy of context streams for the files. Some context information could be acquired from the operating system, such as time and file type. Other information could be gathered from sensors or devices connected to the operating systems, such as location and velocity. It could also be obtained from the internet, such as the weather.

4.4.1.3   Context Description

This module transforms the context information obtained from context acquisition into context description. We define an XML-specification format to describe a file. The context description of a file holds the whole operating history of this file.

4.4.1.4   Context Analysis

This module is not part of the process of context description. It is application-oriented. According to different applications, using various algorithms, we obtain the file list which is useful in the current context.

4.4.1.5   Context Management

Context information in the file description will be rebuilt into the context stream in this module. It manages the relationship between files and context streams.

4.4.2   An MS-Windows-Based Implementation

We implement ScudFile on MS-Windows platform for its popularity. There exist three main issues for our implementation.

4.4.2.1   How to Intercept the File Operations

The tracer component of the ScudFile watches user activities and traces all the file system calls. We use the hook technology to intercept each file system call. We choose the Detours library released by Microsoft, which can detect most of Win32 function calls. We intercept the Win32 functions concerning file operations by rewriting the in-memory code for target functions. Unlike static redirection or DLL relinking, the interception techniques used in the Detours library are guaranteed to work to locate the target function regardless of the method used by application or system code.

```
// give a nick name of system call
DETOUR_TRAMPOLINE(
BOOL WINAPI Trampoline_CopyFile( LPCTSTR lpExistingFileName,
        LPCTSTR lpNewFileName, BOOL bFailIfExists,
        CopyFile);
. . . . . . . . . . . . . . .
//start replace system functions
DetourFunctionWithTrampoline( (PBYTE)Trampoline_CopyFile,
        (PBYTE)Shadow_CopyFile);
. . . . . . . . . . . . . . .
//stop replace system functions
DetourRemoveWithTrampoline( (PBYTE)Trampoline_CopyFile,
        (PBYTE)Shadow_CopyFile);
```

There are two important functions: *DetourFunctionWithTrampoline*, which is used to replace system functions, and *DetourRemoveWithTrampoline*, which is used to remove the replacement. As shown above, the first step is to use the macro of *DETOUR_TRAMPOLINE* to give the system API a nickname, because we should call the function to do the real file operation after our extra work. In the example, we use "*Trampoline_CopyFile*" as the nickname of *CopyFile*, which is the system function for copying files. Then use the *DetourFunctionWithTrampoline* to replace the target function with our function. Now all the system calls of *CopyFile* call the function of *Shadow_CopyFile*. In *Shadow_CopyFile*, we do the task of context acquisition and updating the file description. Before the function returns, we call the *Trampoline_CopyFile* to do the real work of the file copy. From the system function, we can get the file name of the target file. Because we only focus on the user-oriented files, after getting the operation information, we determine whether the target file is user-oriented or not.

4.4.2.2   How to Semantically Describe Files

We need to describe two kinds of information for files, file information and operation information. File information, which usually remains unchanged, contains some static information such as file name and file path. The operation information contains contexts such as operating type, operating time. In our system, we record the whole history of file operations for data analysis. The example shown below demonstrates an operation of file creation. For each operation, there will be a node of "*SF:Action*" to record the operation information. Sometimes, the target file will be operated frequently, such as the action of file saving. For these frequent actions with a short time interval, we merge them into one action.

```
<SF:File>
    <SF:FileUser>qbark</SF:FileUser>
    <SF:FileName>Lecture</SF:FileName>
    <SF:FilePath>F:\Work\</SF:FilePath>
    <SF:FileType>PPT</SF:FileType>
    <SF:FileKeyWord>Meeting</SF:FileKeyWord>
    <SF:Action>
        <SF:OpType>Create</SF:OpType>
        <SF:Time>201002131224</SF:Time>
        <SF:Location>442</SF:location>
        <SF:Weather>Sun</SF:Weather>
    </SF:Action>
<SF:File>
```

4.4.2.3 How to Hasten the Processing of File Context Stream

The extra work introduced by ScudFile will increase the computation cost. We use the technology of multithreading programming to reduce the negative effect. For all the file operations, we create a thread to do the task of context acquisition and file description when a file operation event is detected. In the function of *Shadow_CopyFile*, the extra work includes three aspects: (1) estimate if the target file is user-oriented or not, (2) get the current context information, and (3) describe the target file with context stream.

```
. . . . . . . . . . . .
DWORD ThreadId;
m_hThread = CreateThread( NULL,0,Routine,this,0,&ThreadId );
if( NULL == m_hThread )
{
        CloseHandle( m_hDir );
        m_hDir = INVALID_HANDLE_VALUE;
}
. . . . . . . . . . . .
```

4.5 Applications

Here we introduce three applications based on ScudFile. These applications use the context streams of files to help users find files which may be needed for data analysis.

4.5.1 File Browsing with Context Stream

Most of the current file systems use the tree directory form to organize users' files. Users have to go deeper layer by layer to access a file they want. With the increase in file number, it becomes a boring job [16]. We implement file browsing based on ScudFile in terms of context streams to show files in the form of a virtual directory.

In our implementation, files are mounted in the context stream according to the context of the file operation. From the perspective of a context stream, files are arranged according to the operation time. The files list is not static, but varies with users' file operations. The file accessed recently will appear on the top of the file list.

As shown in Fig. 4.5, files are accessed by choosing the context stream. The leftmost buttons represent the different types of context streams. By clicking the buttons, we can choose a context stream and the system will give detailed

Fig. 4.5 Screenshot of the ScudFile browser

information about the context stream. After a context is selected, for example "home", the list of files which satisfy the conditions will be shown on the right with a virtual directory. All the files listed were operated by the user at home.

4.5.2 File Searching with Context Stream

Different from file searching based on keywords in traditional file managers, ScudFile enables the context information to help the user's searching, as shown in Fig. 4.6. For searching using keywords of the file name or file content, the user needs to keep in mind some information of the target file. With the number of files increasing, it is a burden for users to remember so much information [17]. Users may find it easier to remember the operation context better than the miscellaneous file names, e.g., where the file was modified.

ScudFile has recorded the context of operations. Thus, the user can search the target file through the context of operations, for example weather and location. This application extends the function of a content-based search.

Fig. 4.6 Screenshot of file search in ScudFile. User is choosing the weather context stream as searching condition

4.5.3 File Recommending with Context Stream

Some user behavior is regular, as are file operations. The user often has a similar pattern of file access in a similar environment [18]. For example, a user is accustomed to hearing music after dinner, so in that context he often needs to browse music media files. We could provide these files to the user in advance, enabling users to quickly access them. ScudFile has recorded the history of file operations. From the information of the context stream, we can find the connection between context and file access.

We choose those contexts useful for representing the characteristics of the operation to be integrated in a similarity measure, such as location, time, and file type. Location and time give us the most important environmental information, others such as weather or temperature are not related to the file operation closely. File type and other file attributes tell us which category the file belongs to. We define the similarity between a context and a file using historical information.

$$r = \frac{\sum_i^n x}{\sum_i^n y}$$

Algorithm 4.1 File recommendation algorithm in ScudFile

---

1. Generate of similar intervals and obtain n
2. Search file operations in these intervals in the context stream
3. Count file operations in the first i similar intervals, and get the number pairs: (x, y)
4. Compute the r
5. Merge the results from file type, access time and neighboring rule
6. Output recommendation file list

---

where "n" is the number of the "similar" intervals in the context stream (a similar interval means a maximum continuous segment where all the context values are close to the current context), "y" is the number of file operations in the last i similar intervals, and "x" is the number of file operations for a certain file type in the last i similar intervals. Therefore, the result represents the correlation between the context and file type. Then, to enhance the experience of file recommendation, we merge together the results of the correlated file type, latest access time, and the neighbors of highly correlated files to make a recommendation list (Algorithm 4.1).

4.6 Evaluation

In this section, we present two experiments for evaluation of our system. The first one is the time cost of file operations compared with the original Windows 7. The second evaluation is the usability test of the system.

4.6.1 Time Cost

The current implementation of ScudFile uses the hook technique to detect users' file operations and add context information to the description file. It causes extra computational cost besides file operations. In order to evaluate the difference in time cost between the ScudFile and the original in Windows 7, we carried out four types of file operations, create, copy, rename and delete, with 20,000 times for each operation. The hardware configuration of the desktop computer used in the experiment is Intel Dual Core CPU E5200, 2.5 GHz with 4Gb RAM. The operating system used is Microsoft Windows 7. The result is shown in Fig. 4.7.

From the experimental results, we can see the extra time cost caused by our system is not significant, just a couple of milliseconds for each operation. That means the extra time will not affect users when using the ScudFile. The good performance is mainly attributed to the employment of multithreading technology. When we want to update a file description, we create a new thread.

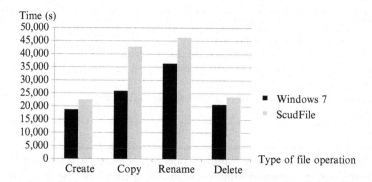

Fig. 4.7 Time cost comparison in the case of 20,000 operations

Table 4.1 Quantitative
evaluation of the usability
(Qn = Question n)

Volunteer	Q1	Q2	Q3	Q4	Q5
A	4	4	5	4	4
B	3	4	4	5	4
C	4	4	4	4	3
D	4	3	5	5	4
E	5	3	4	5	4
Average	4	3.6	4.4	4.6	3.8

4.6.2 Usability Test

To evaluate the user experience of our system, we employed five volunteers to use
our system. After 1 week of usage, we interviewed them to ascertain their opinions
and observations of our system. All the five users were provided with the following
questionnaire in order to get their opinions.

Question 1	I find the system is easy to use.
	1 … 2 … 3 … 4 … 5
Question 2	I find the system is efficient for locating files.
	1 … 2 … 3 … 4 … 5
Question 3	I find the system is easy to learn.
	1 … 2 … 3 … 4 … 5
Question 4	I find the system has no effect on file operation speed.
	1 … 2 … 3 … 4 … 5
Question 5	My overall impression of the ScudFile system.
Very negative	1 … 2 … 3 … 4 … 5 Very positive

Table 4.1 shows the quantitative evaluation results of the five questions. All the
users completed the user experiment and gave their opinions regarding the usability.
From the results, we can learn that the ScudFile has little effect on the speed of file

operations and is easy to use for most of people. The result of Q2 shows that the accuracy of locating files is still a challenge in our system. This will be our main work in the future.

4.7 Conclusion

As individual data files grow, organizational and search tools for file management grow increasingly important. How do we integrate context with files, how do we enhance users' convenience without increasing the burden on users? These become new issues. This chapter presents a context stream to organize files and builds a ScudFile file system integrated with the context stream. It can automatically connect contexts with files by tracing the file system calls. We also implement three applications: file browsing, file searching, file recommendation. The evaluation result demonstrates that the ScudFile is effective in helping personal file management. The idea of association of files with context streams is expected to be integrated into traditional file systems to improve users' experience of personal file management.

References

1. Qiu QJ, Pan G, Shijian L (2010) Modeling files with context streams. In: Yu Z, Liscano R, Chen G, Zhang D, Zhou X (eds) 6th international conference on ubiquitous intelligence and computing, Xi'an, China, Springer, Berlin, Heidelberg, pp 322–336
2. Qiu QJ (2011). ScudFile: context file system based on context stream. Master thesis, Zhejiang University (in Chinese)
3. Ghemawat S, Gobioff H, Leung S-T (2003) The Google file system. SOPSP'03: proceedings of the nineteenth ACM symposium on operating systems principles, Bolton Landing, USA. ACM SIGOPS Oper Syst Rev 37(5):29–43
4. Gifford DK, Jouvelot P, Sheldon MA, O'Toole JW Jr (1991) Semantic file system. 13th ACM symposium on operating system principles, Pacific Grove, USA. ACM SIGOPS Oper Syst Rev 21(5):16–25
5. Hess CK, Campbell RH (2003) An application of a context-aware file system. Pers Ubiquitous Comput 7(6):339–352
6. Gopal B, Manber U (1999) Integrating content-based access mechanisms with hierarchical file system. In: Seltzer MI, Leach PJ (eds) Symposium on operating systems design and implementation, USENIX Association, Berkeley, pp 265–278
7. Norman BS, Adams N, Want R (1994) context-aware computing applications. In: Cabrera L-F, Satyanarayanan M (eds) IEEE workshop on mobile computing systems and application, IEEE Computer Society Press, Santa Cruz, pp 85–90
8. Hess CK, Campbell RH (2003) A context-aware data management system for ubiquitous computing applications. In: 23th international conference on distributed computing system, Providence, RI
9. Roman M, Hess CK, Cerqueira R, Ranganat A, Campbell RH, Nahrstedt K (2002) Gaia: a middleware infrastructure for active space. IEEE Pervasive Comput 1(4):74–83
10. Karypidis A, Lalis S (2007) OmniStore: automating data management in a personal system comprising several portable devices. J Pervasive Mobile Comput 3(5):512–536

11. Karypidis A, Lalis S (2006) OmniStore: a system for ubiquitous personal storage manage-
    ment. In: 4th IEEE international conference on pervasive computing and communications
    (PerCom'06), Pisa, Italy
12. Soules CAN, Ganger GR (2005) Connections: using context to enhance file search. In: 20th
    ACM symposium on operating systems principles, Brighton, UK
13. Dey AK (2001) Understanding and using context. Pers Ubiquitous Comput 5(1):4–7
14. Dey AK, Abowd GD (1999) Towards a better understanding of context and context-awareness.
    Technical report FIT-GVU-99-22, Georgia Institute of Technology
15. Satyanarayanan M, Kistler JJ, Kumar P, Okasaki ME, Siegel EH, Steere DC (1990) Coda: a
    highly available file system for a distributed workstation environment. IEEE Trans Comput
    39(4):447–459
16. Amer A, Long DDE, Paris J-F, Burns RC (2002) File access prediction with adjustable accu-
    racy. In: 21st IEEE international conference on performance, computers and communication,
    Phoenix, AZ
17. Song YJ, Choi YJ, Lee HB, Kim D, Park D (2006) Searchable virtual file system: toward an
    intelligent ubiquitous storage. In: Chung Y-C, Moreira JE (eds) 1st International conference
    advances in grid and pervasive computing, Taiwan. Lecture notes in computer science, vol
    3947, pp 395–404, Springer, Berlin, Heidelberg
18. Lei H, Duchamp D (1997) An analytical approach to prefetching. In: USENIX 1997 annual
    technical conference, Anaheim, CA

Chapter 5
ScudWare: Software Infrastructure for SmartShadow

Abstract Compared with current smart spaces systems (like smart home, and smart office), SmartShadow is quite special. Firstly, unlike a room, it is a highly mobile space. Secondly, it requires frequent information exchange with the outer environment; for instance, it may need local information and other local services. The complexity of SmartShadow needs a software infrastructure of high adaptation to meet complex and easily variational situations. This chapter proposes a semantic and adaptive middleware platform, i.e., ScudWare, for SmartShadowd. In ScudWare, techniques of multi-agent, context-aware and adaptive component management are smoothly synthesized. It consists of three key components: (1) semantic virtual agents; (2) a semantic context management service; and (3) an adaptive component management service. This enables entities in SmartShadow to interact autonomously, provide semantic-integration context awareness, and support component-based adaptability and scalability.

5.1 Introduction

In the twenty-first century, with the rapid development of information technology, a significant revolution is taking place in the computation model. It is an inevitable trend in computation development from distributed computing to ubiquitous computing [1]. There are three essential elements in ubiquitous computing: embedded, small and intelligent devices, multiple kinds of persons, and multiple types of smart spaces. Smart space is a fusion of the physical world and information space, which provides the users with intelligent services and facilities.

To realize the idea of smart space, a lot of information and communication technologies should be developed and integrated into our environment: from toys, desktops to cars, factories and whole city areas with integrated processors, sensors, and actuators connected via wireless high-speed networks and combined with new output devices ranging from projections directly into the eye to large panoramic

Z. Wu and G. Pan, *SmartShadow: Models and Methods for Pervasive Computing*, Advanced Topics in Science and Technology in China, DOI 10.1007/978-3-642-36382-5_5, © Zhejiang University Press, Hangzhou and Springer-Verlag Berlin Heidelberg 2013

displays. Currently, much effort has been made in ubiquitous computing [2–4], especially in smart spaces, e.g., the smart home [5, 6], the aware room [7] and the smart museum [8]. The aware room acts like an invisible butler. It has cameras, microphones, and other sensors and uses these inputs to understand what people are doing in order to help them. It can recognize who is in the room and can interpret his or her hand gestures and the room's interior and knows when drivers are trying to turn, stop, pass, etc., without being told. The smart home aims at creating a living laboratory for research in ubiquitous computing for everyday activities, which has two identical and independent living spaces, consisting of two bedrooms, two bathrooms, one office, a kitchen, one dining room, one living room and one laundry room. In addition, there will be a shared basement with a home entertainment area and control room for centralized computing services. The smart museum is a fertile ground for studying systems to enhance the visitor's experience and tries to improve on this experience with multimedia content. In the smart museum, static and local contents are used on a personal digital assistant (PDA), including a short video clip of the artist explaining his or her work.

In the smart space, users will naturally and transparently interact with each other and with entities in the space, and the space environment can automatically and continuously self-adjust to provide better services for users. Compared with smart spaces addressed before, e.g., meeting room, the SmartShadow is quite special. First, unlike the room, it is a highly mobile space, since the users and devices usually move frequently and rapidly from one place to another. This means that the software infrastructure should support high mobility. Second, the SmartShadow space strongly depends on frequent information exchange with the outer environment; for instance, it may need local traffic information or other local services. This kind of complex environment requires high adaptation of the software infrastructure for smart SmartShadow spaces [9].

We propose a semantic and adaptive middleware platform for SmartShadow space, called ScudWare, where entities have intelligent characters and can adjust themselves adaptively according to their changes to provide high-quality services. ScudWare middleware is based on semantic information and conforms to a lightweight CORBA component model (CCM) specification [10]. The features of ScudWare consist of the following:

(1) Autonomy: ScudWare can dynamically monitor the application environment. Thus, it can interact autonomously, without any user intervention, with the monitored information.
(2) Adaptability: Both the inner running status information and the outer environment context changes can be discerned by ScudWare itself during the run time. In terms of these changes, ScudWare can adaptively modify its inner structure composition and functional behavior.
(3) Scalability: ScudWare is a component-based middleware, and its components can be dynamically added, replaced, and removed. Since a different component composition provides a different service, ScudWare enables its structures and functions to be scalable.

(4) Semantic integration: The semantic information is employed to smoothly manage both presentations and interactions of all entities in SmartShadow for good understanding and collaboration with each other.

5.2 ScudWare Architecture

In order to build the SmartShadow space naturally and adaptively, we develop a semantic and adaptive middleware platform called ScudWare based on the adaptive communication environment (ACE) [11], the ACE ORB (TAO) [12], and embedded operating systems. TAO is a real-time object request broker developed by Washington University, St. Louis, MO. In ScudWare, the multi-agent technique is also employed to construct SVAs for SmartShadow.

Our proposed ScudWare middleware is built on the basis of embedded systems, ACE, and TAO, as shown in Fig. 5.1. Embedded systems such as SmartOSEK [13, 14], embedded Linux, Win CE, are implemented on embedded microprocessors and are enabled to take off real-time tasks. The embedded operating systems often contain four components: (1) task management, (2) scheduling, (3) resource management, and (4) interrupt handling, to provide the essential functions for high-level ScudWare middleware services. ACE [11] can use J1939, CAN-Open, TCP/IP and wireless protocols to provide high-performance and real-time communications for ScudWare middleware. It uses interprocess communication, event demultiplexing, explicit dynamic linking and concurrency. ACE simplifies the

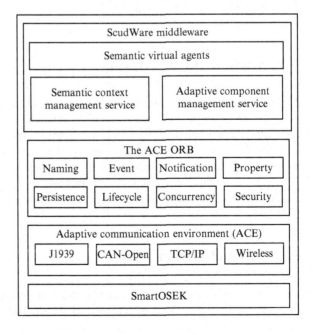

Fig. 5.1 Architecture of ScudWare

development of object-oriented network applications and services in the ScudWare middleware. TAO is an ACE ORB that uses the best software patterns on ACE in order to automate the delivery of high-performance and real-time quality of service (QoS) to distributed applications. It includes basic services such as naming, event, notification, property, persistence, concurrency, lifecycle, and security service to support the cooperation of SVAs, an SCMS and an ACMS of the ScudWare middleware. The ScudWare architecture [15] is shown in Fig. 5.1, which consists of three components. It can be defined as

$$ScudWare = (SVA, SCMS, ACMS) \tag{5.1}$$

(1) SVA denotes a semantic virtual agent. Each application in SmartShadow will be decomposed into several task units, and then some SVAs are chosen to deal with each task. The role of the SVA is an abstract function union that comprises a number of meta-objects. The interactions of SVAs are autonomous. The meta-object denotes a kind of service comprising several components. SVA uses the naming, event, notification, and property services of TAO.
(2) SCMS denotes a semantic context management service that is a semantic-integration service, including context acquisition, representation, and fusion. SCMS uses the property, persistence, and concurrency services of TAO.
(3) ACMS denotes an adaptive component management service that has two parts: (1) component package, assembly, deployment, and allocation at design time; and (2) component migration, replacement, updating, and variation at run time. Using these component management methods, ScudWare middleware achieves adaptability and scalability. ACMS uses the naming, event, notification, lifecycle, and security services of TAO.

5.3   Semantic Virtual Agents

Multi-agent architectures and methodologies for adaptation have been conducted [16, 17]. In order to deal with complex dynamic environments of ubiquitous computing, some solutions based on agent-level adaptation have been proposed [18–20]. Compared with them, we focus on the agent model that enables flexible structure level and run-time adaptation based on semantic information to meet the ubiquitous computing environments and variant run-time contexts. In this section, we present the SVA and its Semantic Interface Protocol (SIP).

5.3.1   SVA Definition

For each application from SmartShadow, we first decompose it into several task units. Then, a set of SVAs is selected for each task. The role of SVA is an abstract

Fig. 5.2 SVAs in ScudWare

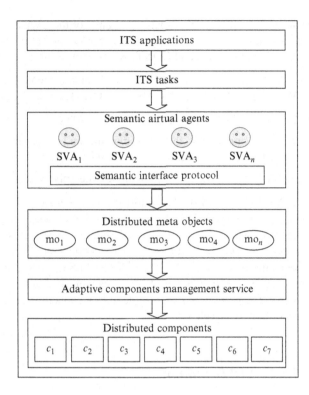

function union that comprises of a number of meta objects. The meta object is a kind of service comprising several components. Thus, the basic element of SVA is the "component." We use a component manager to administer distributed components, which form the meta objects for cooperation and communication.

Figure 5.2 illustrates the SVA. For instance, an application AP consists of two tasks, namely t_1 and t_2. Task t_1 requires SVA_1, SVA_2, and SVA_3, and task t_2 needs SVA_2 and SVA_3. SVA_1 consists of mo_1 and mo_2. SVA_2 comprises mo_2 and mo_3. SVA_3 is made up of mo_3 and mo_4. The component manager is responsible for finding the best components to form the meta objects. The formal definitions of AP and SVA are as follows.

Definition 5.1. The user application AP is defined as AP = (SE,TA), where SE is a semantic information set of the application, and TA is a task set decomposed from the application. According to the different application demands, these tasks have different temporal logic relationships. Each task comprises three required properties: name priority, and complexity.

Definition 5.2. SVA is defined as SVA = (CP, TASK, MO, KB, TB, SQ∪RQ), where CP is a set of SVAs' capabilities denoted as CP = cp_1, cp_2, cp_3,..., cp_n. It is emphasized that each cp_i is one minimal unit of the SVA's capabilities. Each SVA has the ability to append, modify, delete, or find its capabilities according to the different contexts. The capability change of the SVA is defined as $\triangle \text{CP} = \text{OP}(\text{CP}, \text{CONTEXT})$, where OP is a set of SVAs' operations denoted as $\text{OP} = \text{append}$, modify, delete, find, and CONTEXT is a set of run-time environments information.

MO is a set of meta objects to form the SVA. KB is a knowledge base of SVA, i.e., $\text{KB} = \text{kb}_1, \text{kb}_2, \text{kb}_3, \ldots, \text{kb}_n$. Each kb is a set of rules and rule= $\bigcup_{i=1}^{n} (m_i, \text{interface}(m_i), \text{key}, \text{lifetime}, \text{sp}_i)$, where m_i is a set of recently cooperating missions. Importantly, the rule is dynamic and self-updating when the related events happen or some conditions are satisfied. TB is a trust policy base, i.e., $\text{TB} = \bigcup_{i=1}^{n} (\text{SVA}_i, \text{TM}(\text{SVA}_i))$, which includes the trust security rules for cooperation of SVAs. $\text{TM}(x) = (\text{trustvalue}, \text{priority}, \text{prestige}, \text{history})$ is a trust evaluation function. $\text{RQ} = \bigcup \text{Msg}$ and $\text{SQ} = \bigcup \text{Msg}$ are two sets of messages processing queues, which are responsible for receiving and sending messages separately, and $\text{Msg} = \text{req}$, accept, refuse, $\ldots$, msgn. Several SVAs cooperate to fulfill each task ta_i, which is formalized as $\forall \text{ta} \in \text{TA} \rightarrow \bigcup_{1 < x,y < P}^{1 < i,j < Q} \exists \text{SVA}_i, \text{SVA}_j \in \text{SVA} \cdot R(\text{SVA}_i \cdot \text{cp}_x, \text{SVA}_j \cdot \text{cp}_y, c)$. P is the maximum number of SVAs' capabilities, and Q is the maximum number of SVAs. The prediction $R(a,b,c)$ denotes a cooperative relationship between a and b according to the rule c.

5.3.2   SIP Definition

For SVAs cooperation, we have defined a few key principles to form the SPI set. They are SVA discovery, join, lease, and self-updating protocols, as illustrated in Fig. 5.3.

(1) The SVA discovery protocol allows an SVA to find another required SVA without a fixed naming SVA service. There are two discovery models: peer-to-peer model [(model (a)] and multicast model [model (b)]. If SVA_1 demands a capability c_1 and knows that SVA_2 has cp_1, SVA_1 will use model (a) and send a request message to SVA_2 for direct communication. Otherwise, if SVA_1 does not know who has cp_1, SVA_1 will take model (b). SVA_1 first sends a multicast request message m to other SVAs. Assume that SVA_n has cp_1 and receives m. If SVA_1 is authenticated by SVA_n, SVA_n will send a reply message to SVA_1. Finally, they begin to cooperate with trust.

(2) The SVA join protocol allows an SVA to take part in and leave an SVA community. For example, assume that an SVA community sc_1 comprises SVA_4, SVA_6, and SVA_8, where they cooperate directly and with trust. If SVA_2 comes and wants to join sc_1, it is firstly required to get authentication from all the members of sc_1, and then it can act as a member of sc_1. Once SVA_2 leaves the community sc_1, SVA_2 will be regarded as a nontrusted member. It needs to be authenticated again when cooperation is required.

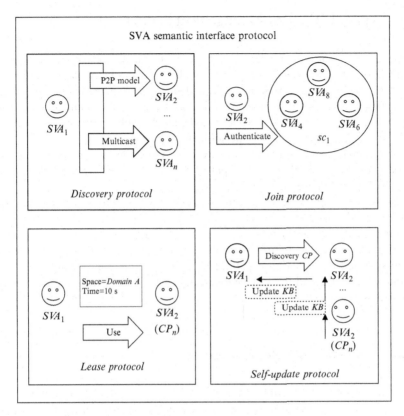

Fig. 5.3 Semantic interface protocol for SVAs

(3) The SVA lease protocol defines the space and time principles during SVAs' cooperation. For example, if SVA_1 requires a capability cp_n of SVA_2 and is authenticated by SVA_2, SVA_1 and SVA_2 will negotiate the usage restriction of cp_n. Assume that the results are that space = Domain A and time = 10s, which means SVA_1 can use cp_n just in Domain A for 10s. If SVA_1 wants to continue using cp_n after the time expires, SVA_1 should relet cp_n with SVA_2.

(4) The SVA self-update protocol defines the principle of SVA KB updating. SVA_1 requires a capability cp_n to get one system parameter. According to its KB, SVA_1 first finds that SVA_2 has cp_n. Then, SVA_1 sends a request message to SVA_2. If SVA_2 still has cp_n, they will cooperate after authentication. Otherwise, if SVA_2 currently has no cp_n, SVA_2 will search the other SVA which has cp_n according to its KB and update the KB at the same time. This process will continue until one SVA having cp_n is found or no some SVA is found.

5.4   Semantic Context Management Service

Context is any information that can be used to characterize the status of an entity [21]. An entity may be a person, a place, or an object that is considered relevant to the interaction between a user and an application, including the user and application themselves. Commonly used contexts consist of location, identity, time, temperature, and activity. We consider that the involved objects in environments are all contexts. Context awareness is the ability to sense and use different contexts. Any application that takes advantage of context is a context-aware application. Context-aware computing is the ability of computing devices to detect, interpret, and respond to changes in the environment and the system.

The semantic information of contexts is essential for dealing with the complex tasks in ubiquitous computing environments. However, representing sharing and reasoning of the contexts is very difficult. In smart spaces, context is hard to represent and use due to its complexity. It requires an approach with strong expression and easy sharing capabilities. In this section, we attempt to use the ontology technique and the web ontology language (OWL) from the field of the semantic web to solve the problem.

5.4.1   Semantic View for Context

As Berners-Lee and Fischetti [22] have described, the semantic web is an extension of the current web where information is given a well-defined meaning. The semantic web is a vision where web pages are augmented with information and data expressed in a way that facilitates its understanding by computing machines. The goal of the semantic web initiatives sponsored by the World Wide Web Consortium (W3C) is to develop languages that are adequate for representing and reasoning the semantics of information on the web. The semantic web provides an infrastructure that enables not just web pages but databases, services, programs, sensors, personal devices, and even household appliances to both consume and produce data on the web. The W3C organization has specified a language OWL [23] that is based on DAML and OIL for the semantic web, which is more expressive than RDF and RDF-S [24]. The OWL language builds on XML's ability to define customized tagging schemes and RDF's flexible approach to represent data. The semantic web technologies and OWL language are suitable for dealing with the complex contexts in smart spaces.

The semantic view of context is to use the aforementioned semantic technologies to manage the context. Firstly, the context ontology of the application domain should be built using OWL language as a standard syntax. Secondly, we can share the common vocabularies of the contexts. Finally, we can represent context information and inference more effectively and adaptively than we do nowadays.

5.4.2 Ontology of SmartShadow Space

An ontology [25] is an agreement about a shared conceptualization, which includes the conceptual frameworks for modeling application domain knowledge, content-specific protocols for communication among interacting agents, and agreements about the representation of specific domain theories. Ontology has characteristics such as definitions of representational vocabulary, a well-defined syntax, easily understood semantics, efficient reasoning support, sufficient expressive capabilities, and convenience of expression.

The common understanding of ontology is on two levels. (1) It is a vocabulary that uses appropriate terms to describe entities and relationships between entities. (2) It is a knowledge base for a specific domain.

In our opinion, an ontology describes the domain knowledge in a general way and provides consistent understanding of one application domain. Here, we describe ontology building and ontology usage in SmartShadow.

(1) Ontology Building. SmartShadow is a special environment, we examine the characteristics from the view of semantic context. To build the ontology in the SmartShadow easily, we give two principles: (1) The space inside a space is relatively confined. The devices inside it are limited and fixed. In addition, the space for users to move in is restricted. (2) Although environments outside a space change continually, we need not concern with all dynamic changes. What we need is only those that can influence our special applications.

Based on the two principles, we have built an ontology of SmartShadow, i.e.,

$$Ontology_{svs} = Oenv, Ousr, Oveh \tag{5.2}$$

where Oenv is a set of the environmental contexts that may influence the user's life such as weather information, environmental status and events. Ousr is a set of the user's contexts including (1) the status of the user such as the career and education level and (2) the physiological parameters such as alcohol level and pupil diameter. Oveh is a set of the system contexts including the status of the inside-space devices such as air conditioner, wiper, light, engine, antilock braking system (ABS), and seat.

We have used the Protégé [26] tool to build this ontology and create some instances in a SmartShadow. Protégé is an ontology editor tool that provides a graphical user interface for users to create and manage the ontology architecture easily. Using this tool, we can export files in OWL format for further reasoning. One screenshot is shown in Fig. 5.4.

(2) Ontology Usage. We have built an ontology and defined three base classes that, respectively, represent the context inside the SmartShadow, the outside environment of the space, and the user. In order to be able to rely on the knowledge base, we filter the context scenario and specify fixed conditions that

Fig. 5.4 Ontology created
by protégé

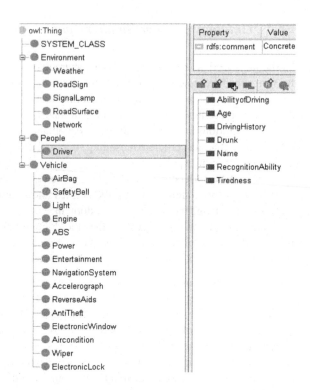

trigger specific actions. Once the system meets the condition we have defined, the context reasoning system will be triggered and will perform the associated actions. Herein, we use a scenario of driving to illustrate usage of ontology.

The context scenarios that we are interested in comprise three parts, which are defined as $IS = (SD,OI,DR)$, where SD is a set of the security driving, including the scenario of driving at high speed in case of emergency; OI is a set of influences of the outside environment, such as the vehicle can follow the road sign or the ABS will engage in the case of loss of traction; and DR is a set of the driver status.

We specify several driver conditions. Each one corresponds to different physiological parameters. The system takes various actions according to different danger levels. For example, if the driver is unable to continue driving when the danger level is high, the system will force a controlled stop and call for help. If the condition is not so serious, the system may simply park at the nearest convenient location. As a result, with the ontology, the system can deal with different problems adaptively.

(3) Reasoning Using OWL. When taking the ontology approach to model context, we can process context with logical reasoning mechanisms. We use a context reasoning method to deduce high-level implicit contexts from low-level explicit contexts. Ontological reasoning is a rule base consisting of the predefined rules that can reason about OWL vocabularies and new concepts. Rules are

Table 5.1 Some OWL ontology reasoning rules

	Reasoning rules
inverseOf	$(?P_1 \, owl : inverseOf \,?P_2) \wedge (?X\,?P_1\,?Y) \Rightarrow (?Y\,?P_2\,?X)$
TransitiveProperty	$(?P\,rdf : type\,owl : TransitiveProperty) \wedge (?X\,?P\,?Y) \wedge (?Y\,?P\,?Z) \Rightarrow (?X\,?P\,?Z)$
SymmetricProperty	$(?P\,rdf : type\,owl : SymmetricProperty) \wedge (?X\,?P\,?Y) \Rightarrow (?Y\,?P\,?X)$
differentForm	$(?P_1 \, owl : differentFrom\,?P_2) \wedge (?X\,rdf : type\,?P_1) \wedge (?Y\,rdf : type\,?P_2)$
	$\Rightarrow (?X\,owl : differentFrom\,?Y)$
subClassOf	$(?X\,rdfs : subClassOf\,?Y) \wedge (?Y\,rdfs : subClassOf\,?Z) \Rightarrow (?X\,rdfs : subClassOf\,?Z)$
subPropertyOf	$(?\alpha\,rdfs\,subPropertyOf\,?\beta) \wedge (?\beta\,rdfs : subPropertyOf\,?\gamma) \Rightarrow (?\alpha\,rdfs : subPropertyOf\,?\gamma)$

constructed with two properties, namely action and condition. Action is a statement representing what shall be done if the condition is satisfied. Condition in one rule is a collection of statements. Condition is satisfied if all of its component statements are satisfied.

First-order predicates are used to implement context reasoning. The structure of the first-order predicate has three parts, a subject, an object; and a verb. For example, the physical location context "Wu sits in the driver's seat" can be described as (Wu, Sit, Driver Seat). We can use this description logic (DL) to embody OWL-Lite entailed semantics. Table 5.1 illustrates a subset of reasoning rules that support these semantics.

For example, in the context ontology building described in the previous section, we define an OWL: TransitiveProperty relation-locatedIn, denoting that one context entity locates in one place. We also define an OWL: subClassOf relation denoting that one class is a subclass of another. According to the OWL ontology reasoning rules and some contexts that are already acquired, we can conduct the OWL ontology reasoning with some scenarios in smart vehicle space. First, explicit context is acquired from some related sensors directly, whereas implicit context is the additional information deduced from explicit context. In this case, Mr. Wu currently sits in the driver's seat, which is located in the smart car, and the smart car is on the Shanghai–Hangzhou Highway. In addition, the J1939, which is one of the ACEs, is used in the smart car for electronic control unit (ECU) communications, and ACE is one of the networks. Then, we use DL and OWL ontology rules to conclude that Mr. Wu is on the Shanghai–Hangzhou Highway. J1939 is one of the networks.

5.4.3 Semantic Context Service Functional Modules

According to the semantic view for context and ontology of SmartShadow, we present a semantic context model and integrate it into ScudWare middleware, which is responsible for context adaptive management, including context acquisition, representation and fusion. In particular, semantic context model is based on semantic information using semantic web and ontology technologies. In addition, a semantic

Fig. 5.5 Semantic context
service functional modules

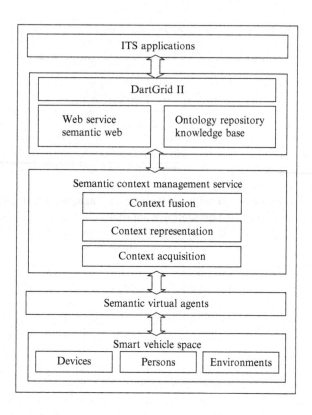

context model can cooperate with SVA on the multiagent level in the semantic web. ScudWare also provides interfaces to access DartGrid II [27], which is a semantic grid platform for ITS. The function of SCMS is shown in Fig. 5.5. We introduce the three functional modules of this model.

(1) Context Acquisition: This is a low-layer module in the model. Many kinds of sensors such as temperature, speed, and humidity sensors are used to obtain the low-level and coarse sensing data for further processing. For example, the temperature sensor can measure the temperature inside or outside the space; the digital cameras, microphone, and physiologic sensors are used to get the status of people; and the air sensor is used to detect alcohol and toxic gases. Notice that the data from this part have low-level semantic meaning and are not to be shared and used. Therefore, the data need to be well represented.

(2) Context Representation: In order to share well and use the low-level context data from the context acquisition part, we need to make the data well understood. For high-level semantic abstraction, we use a semantic web language and OWL language to represent these data in terms of the ontology associated with SmartShadow. The ontology repository is built to represent and understand the data better. For example, we can represent the speed of the vehicle, driver's tiredness level, and road surface status for easy understanding and utilization based on ontology.

(3) Context Fusion: Based on the semantic context information from context representation, the problem of context sharing and understanding is coped with. However, the contexts should be further processed, including fusion and inference, to decide which actions will be taken. In this part, the useless contexts are removed and the useful information is for reasoning based on the knowledge base. After the context fusion, the decisions are made and some actions are executed. Here, the context information is dynamic and hierarchical.

5.5 Adaptive Component Management Service

In this section, we describe the ACMS in a structural method. Because the component management is resource constrained, we first give a resource abstract and then detail this service.

5.5.1 Resource Abstract

The goal of the resource abstract is to support component adaptation [28] in ScudWare middleware. In refining this goal, two requirements of ScudWare should be identified. (1) The ScudWare must be extensible to capture diverse types of resources at different levels of abstraction, including the central processing unit processing resources (e.g., threads and virtual processors), memory resources (e.g., random access memory and disk storage), communication resources (e.g., network bandwidth and transport connections), OS resources (e.g., Windows, Linux, and Unix), and component container resources (e.g., CCM, EJB, and .Net). (2) The ScudWare must provide maximum control to applications according to resource adaptation.

A resource is a run-time entity that offers a service for which one needs to express a measure of QoS. In SmartShadow, various smart devices provide resources on different levels. Also, a large number of components are distributed on these devices, consuming computation resources during execution. Since the joining and removal of the smart devices and components are dynamic, they form a relationship between the producer and the consumer based on computation resources. For instance, when a new smart device d goes into a system S, the components in S can use the resources provided by d. When a new component c enters a system S, it will decide how to allocate c automatically and adaptively. In particular, component c can migrate from one device to another.

The resource abstract could be written as

$$RA = (DM, RM, CM, TM, PS) \qquad (5.3)$$

where DM is a smart device manager that monitors the device lifetime, type, and energy and provides a mechanism for universal plug and play devices. RM Resource manager that administers resource lifecycle, type, quantity and allocation. CM: ACMS that is responsible for component lifecycle, allocation, QoS and context management. TM: Task manager that decomposes the application into several tasks based on semantic information (TM monitors tasks' lifetime and schedules them in an adaptive way). PS: Set of management policies that is well defined for dynamic reconfiguration.

5.5.2   ACMS Functionality

With the resource abstract mechanics, an ACMS is developed. This service is responsible for allocating and reallocating the components in an appropriate manner. It monitors the component lifetime and conducts the QoS of component execution. Notice that this service uses a run-time component hook proxy, which is described in the next section.

In a component lifecycle, there are two kinds of key behavior component migration and component replication. Both kinds of behavior are essential for adaptive component management. Because the components are distributed in such a dynamic and discrete system, this service should adaptively take measures about when and how to migrate or replicate components.

Components are installed in various smart devices. Component migration means moving one component from one device to another. The former device will not hold that component, and the latter device becomes the new resource carrier for that component. Emphatically stated, the latter device should have suitable resources for that component, including necessary hardware resources, OS resources and component container resources.

Component replication means copying a component from one device to another. In component replication, unlike component migration, the former still has that component. As a result, there are two of the same components in two different devices. Also, both devices should have suitable resources for that component.

To illustrate the two kinds of behavior, we give the case shown in Fig. 5.6. At first, component c_1 is distributed in smart device d_1, and d_1 also has components c_2 and c_3. Assuming that c_2 is executing and occupies more hardware resources of d_1, it is duduced that c_1 cannot be executed for limited hardware resources when one invocation comes. Under this condition, the component management service will decide to migrate c_1 to another device d_2. Next, at some appropriate time, the component migration of c_1 will take place. Following that, c_1 will be executed on d_2 successfully.

Another case of component replication is as follows: Originally, c_4 is distributed in smart device d_3. Different from the former case, the number of invocations of c_4 is very large. For load balance, the component manger will decide to copy c_4 to

Fig. 5.6 ACMS functionality and a case

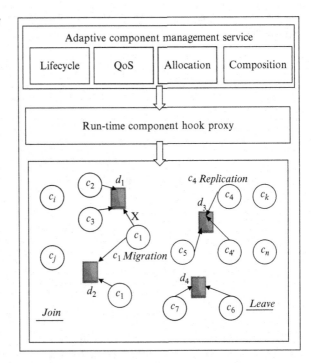

another device. Assuming that d_4 is satisfied with the resource demands of c_4 and is not busy at that time, $c_{4'}$, which is the backup of c_4, will be distributed in d_4 to decrease the invocations of c_4 in d_3.

5.5.3 Component Interdependence Graph

During component management, the relationships among components are very important. In order to describe the interdependent relationships among components, we introduce a component interdependence graph composed of component nodes and link paths.

Each component is associated with a node. Also, the link path is labeled with a weight. We define the component interdependence graph $A_{ig} = (\mathrm{CN}, \mathrm{LP}, W)$, where $\mathrm{CN} = \mathrm{cn}_i i = 1, \ldots, n$ denotes a set of component nodes. $\mathrm{LP} = l_{i,j}, i = 1, \ldots, n; j = 1, \ldots, m$ denotes a set of component links describing the dependent targets. $l_{i,j}$ is the link between the nodes cn_i and cn_j. $W = w_{i,j} i = 1, \ldots, n; j = 1, \ldots, m$ denotes a set of interdependent weights. $w_{i,j}$ is a nonnegative real number, which labels $l_{i,j}$.

The weight $w_{i,j}$ reflects the importance of the interdependence between the associated components. These weights are used, for instance, to detect which link becomes too heavy or if the systems rely too much on some components. In terms of the weight, we can decide which component should be allocated preferentially.

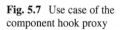
Fig. 5.7 Use case of the
component hook proxy

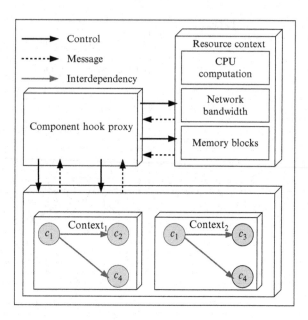

This graph keeps on changing when the contexts vary. Therefore, the interdependence is not static. It will be updated when a new component is added or a component disappears. Moreover, when the application domain contexts and the run-time environments change, the interdependent relationships will also vary.

5.5.4 Run-Time Component Hook Proxy

Generally, in a large and complex ubiquitous computing environment, most resources are limited. Software components are distributed and connected and frequently communicate with each other. However, some relationships are temporary, and some are perpetual, which means that the components do not always depend on certain components for cooperation. Therefore, we use the component interdependence graph to describe run-time component self-adaptation.

During execution time, the dynamic interdependence graph is generated automatically by the component hook proxy that is responsible for acquiring information to analyze and update the interdependence graph to manage the component lifetime.

Under the change in contexts, the component hook proxy uses different strategies. A simple example of a mobile music system is shown in Fig. 5.7. There are four components for the mobile music system, c_1, c_2, c_3, and c_4. Component c_1 is responsible for acquiring music information, component c_2 is for playing music in stereo, component c_3 is for playing music in mono, and component c_4 is for outputting the music. At first, the network bandwidth is enough, and the component hook proxy selects c_1, c_2, and c_4 to deal with the task and forms a component interdependence graph. However, when the component hook proxy finds that the network bandwidth is scarce and cannot transmit a stereo track successfully, it will stop the action of c_2 and then choose c_3 to replace c_2. After that, the component interdependence graph also changes.

5.6 Conclusion

SmartShadow poses a number of new challenges for middleware technology. In particular, such user-centered ubiquitous computing environments may require a semantic and adaptive middleware architecture to trustfully communicate, operate resources, manage data, and provide various services for real-time space responding. Increasingly, adaptive middleware is playing a more important role for ubiquitous computing in smart space. The correctness of middleware adaptation is a key problem. We present ScudWare, which is a semantic and adaptive middleware platform for SmartShadow in ubiquitous computing environments. The ScudWare middleware is based on embedded operating systems and an ACE. We have improved the TAO services and developed an SCMS and an ACMS. We mainly present an adaptation semantic specification framework, consisting of context-aware adaptation temporal logic, two context-aware adaptation semantic specifications, and three composition operations on adaptation semantic specifications, to ensure the adaptation is efficient and reliable. We achieve the synchronization and the adaptability aspects of SmartShadow at the multi-agent, context-aware and adaptive component level according to the semantic information.

References

1. Weiser M (1991) The computer for the 21st century. Sci Am 265(3):66–75
2. Davies N, Gellersen HW (2002) Beyond prototypes: challenges in deploying ubiquitous systems. IEEE Pervasive Comput 1(1):26–35
3. Kindberg T, Fox A (2002) System software for ubiquitous computing. IEEE Pervasive Comput 1(1):70–81
4. Beresford A, Kall CK, Kretschmer U, Mattern F, Muehlenbrock M (2003) The first summer school on ubiquitous and pervasive computing. IEEE Pervasive Comput 2(1):84–88
5. MIT Media Lab. Smart room (1995) [Online]. Available: http://vismod.www.media.mit.edu/vismod/demos/smartroom/. Retrieved 21 Dec 2012
6. MIT Media Lab. Kids room (1997) [Online]. Available: http://vismod.www.media.mit.edu/vismod/demos/kidsroom/. Retrieved 21 Dec 2012
7. Georgia Tech. Aware home project (2001) [Online]. Available: http://www.cc.gatech.edu/fce/ahri/. Retrieved 21 Dec 2012
8. Fleck M, Frid M, Kindberg T, O'Brien-Strain E, Rajani R, Spasojevic M (2002) From informing to remembering: ubiquitous systems in interactive museums. IEEE Pervasive Comput 1(2):13–21
9. Tripathi A (2002) Next-generation middleware systems challenges designing. Commun ACM 45(6):39–42

10. The Object Management Group (OMG®) (2005) CORBA component model (CCM) specification [Online]. Available: http://www.omg.org/technology/documents/formal/components.htm. Retrieved 21 Dec 2012
11. Schmidt DC (2005) Washington University in St. Louis, ACE: the adaptive communication environment [Online]. Available: http://www.cs.wustl.edu/~schmidt/ACE.html. Retrieved 21 Dec 2012
12. Schmidt DC (2005) Washington University in St. Louis TAO: the ACE ORB. [Online]. Available: http://www.cs.wustl.edu/~schmidt/TAO.html. Retrieved 21 Dec 2012
13. Zhao MD, Wu ZH, Yang GQ, Wang L, Chen W (2004) SmartOSEK: a dependable platform for automobile electronics. In: Wu Z, Chen C, Guo M, Bu J (eds) Proceedings of 1st international conference of embedded software and systems, Hangzhou, PR China, Springer, vol. 3605, pp 355–365
14. OSEK/VDX:OSEK/VDX Operating System Specification Version 2.2.3. (2005, Feb 17) [Online]. Available http://portal.osek-vdx.org/files/pdf/specs/os223.pdf
15. Wu ZH, Wu Q, Cheng H, Pan G, Zhao MD, Sun J (2007) ScudWare: a semantic and adaptive middleware platform for smart vehicle space. IEEE Trans Intell Transp Syst 8(1):121–132
16. Ferber J, Gutknecht O, Aladin (1998) A meta-model for the analysis and design of organizations in multi-agent systems. In: Demazeau Y (ed) Proceedings of the international conference on multi agent systems, IEEE Press, pp 128–135
17. Wooldridge M, Jennings N, Kinny D (1999) The methodology Gaia for agent-oriented analysis and design. Artif Intell 10(2):1–27
18. Carley KM (1998) Organizational adaptation. Ann Oper Res 75:25–47
19. Odell J (2002) Agents and complex systems. J Object Technol 1(2):35–45
20. Guessoum Z, Ziane M, Faci N (2004) Monitoring and organizational-level adaptation of multi-agent systems. In: Brueckner S, Di Marzo Serugendo G, Karageorgos A, Nagpal R (eds) Proceedings of the international conference on autonomous agents and multi agent systems. ACM Press, New York, pp 514–520
21. Dey AK (2000) Providing architectural support for building context-aware applications. PhD dissertation, Georgia Institute of Technology, Atlanta, GA
22. Berners-Lee T, Fischetti M (2001) Weaving the web: the original design and ultimate destiny of the World Wide Web by its inventor. Harper, San Francisco
23. Web Ontology Working Group (2004, Feb) OWL web ontology language overview [Online]. Available http://www.w3.org/2004/OWL/
24. RDF Core Working Group (2004, Feb) RDF primer [Online]. Available http://www.w3.org/RDF/
25. Chandrasekaran B, Josephson J R, Benjamins RV (1999) What are ontologies, and why do we need them?. IEEE Intell Syst 14(1):20–26
26. Natalya FN, Michael S, Stefan D, Monica C, Ray WF, Mark AM (2001) Creating semantic web contents with protege-2000. IEEE Intell Syst 16(2):60–71
27. Wu ZH, Deng SG, Wu J, et al (2005) DartGrid II: a semantic grid platform for ITS. IEEE Intell Syst 20(3):12–18
28. Duran-Limon HA, Blair GS, Coulson G (2004) Adaptive resource management in middleware: a survey. IEEE Distributed Syst 5(7):1–13

Chapter 6
Smart Car Space: An Application

Abstract Smart cars are a promising application domain for ubiquitous computing. In the highly mobile car, it is a challenging task to provide a comfortable, convenient, nonintrusive, and safe space that can ubiquitously access information and service. This chapter presents a general framework of smart car space from the point of view of context-awareness. A specific context model is proposed for describing both simple and complex context in smart car space. A driver behavior model for a smart car is proposed for comfortable car-following and multi-task processing. A smart car space prototype is built for demonstration and verification.

6.1 Introduction

People use the car so frequently that it can be regarded as a personal private space, an extension of a personal house. It is valuable to provide people with a comfortable, convenient, nonintrusive, and safe space in the car. For the car industry, a key goal is to improve safety. Typical examples are such devices as air bags, ABS-brakes, and seat belts. In the automation and computer science community, much research focuses on autonomous driving. A famous system is CMU Navlab [1], steering autonomously for 98 % of a 3,000 miles trip from Pittsburgh to San Diego. However, it is still very difficult to put it into practice. New technologies are likely to complement rather than replace the driver, such as Siemens' Night Vision System and Park Mate [2]. Pentland's SmartCar [3] focused on inferring human intentions by their actions in order to enhance interaction. Siewiorek's work [4] addressed providing a multimodal interface for a driver mainly based on vision. An appealing way, also very challenging, is to build a ubiquitous computing environment inside the car, which is not completely investigated yet.

Compared with smart spaces addressed before, e.g., meeting room or house, the SmartCar space is quite particular. (1) It is a highly mobile space, since vehicles move from one place to another frequently and rapidly. This means that the system

Z. Wu and G. Pan, *SmartShadow: Models and Methods for Pervasive Computing*, Advanced Topics in Science and Technology in China, DOI 10.1007/978-3-642-36382-5_6, © Zhejiang University Press, Hangzhou and Springer-Verlag Berlin Heidelberg 2013

should support its high mobility. (2) The vehicle space strongly depends on frequent information exchanging with the outer environment, and the information service is very prominent. For instance, it may need local traffic information or other local services. This kind of complex environment requires adaptation of the infrastructure. (3) The Smart car space generally is much smaller than other spaces. Much mechanical equipment and many electronic devices are distributed compactly in the car, while human activities and resources are highly constrained. (4) The driver needs to keep his/her eyes on the road when driving, which makes the system's interaction with drivers very different from other spaces.

A typical scenario can be described as below. It's time for John and his wife Jenny to go to work. They work in the same place. When John gets in their car, the active camera detects his identity via a face. Then, the car space loads his profile and preference, and the car speakers begins to send the background music that just now played in his home with his preferred music volume. Meanwhile, the car begins to provide information that he is mostly interested in via speech synthesis, e.g., weather forecast, information on stocks that John holds, IT companies' news that John knows. Jenny is busy checking emails and modifying her schedule using PDA. All the data will transparently synchronize with the data in her office. While John is driving, the car reminds him to buy a birthday gift for his daughter as he approaches a big toyshop. When they discuss the gift, the car automatically perceives the discussion and reduces the background music volume to a low level. When their talking stops, the music returns to the normal level. When the car nears the office building, a map of the empty parking positions is shown on the monitor.

6.2   Smart Car Space: A Framework

A smart car space is a comprehensive framework integrated with many different networks, sensors, control modules, actuators, services, and so on [5, 6]. A smart car space can monitor the driving environment, assess the possible risks and take appropriate actions to avoid or reduce the risk. A general architecture of a smart car space [7] is shown in Fig. 6.1.

(1) Traffic monitoring. A variety of scanning technologies can be used to recognize the distance between the car and other road users. Active environment-sensing inside and outside of the car will be a general capability in near future [8]. Lidar, radar, or vision-based approaches can be used to provide the positioning information. The radar and lidar sensors provide information about the relative position and relative velocity of an object. Multiple cameras are able to eliminate blind spots, recognize obstacles, and record the surroundings. Besides the sensing technology described above, the car can get traffic information from the internet or nearby cars.

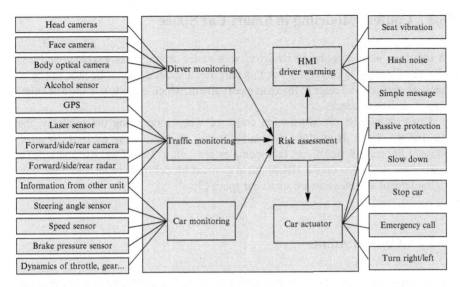

Fig. 6.1 The general architecture of a smart car space

(2) Driver monitoring. Drivers represent the highest safety risk. Almost 95 % of the accidents are due to human factors and in almost three-quarters of the cases human behavior is solely to blame [9]. Smart cars present promising potential to assist drivers in improving their situational awareness and reducing errors. With cameras monitoring the driver's gaze and activity, smart cars attempt to keep the driver's attention on the road ahead. Physiological sensors can detect whether the driver is in good condition.

(3) Car monitoring. The dynamics of a car can be read from the engine, the throttle and the brake. These data will be transferred by controller area networks (CAN) in order to analyze whether the car functions normally.

(4) Risk assessment. It determines the risk of the driving task according to the driver behavior model and situation of traffic, driver, and car. Different levels of risk will lead to different responses, including notifying the driver through HMI (human machine interface) and taking emergency actions by car actuators.

(5) HMI driven warning. It warns the driver of the potential risks in non-emergent situations. For example, a fatigued driver would be awakened by an acoustic alarm or vibrating seat. Visual indications should be applied in a cautious way, since a complex graph or long text sentence will seriously impair the driver's attention and possibly cause harm.

(6) Car actuator. The actuators will execute specified control of the car without the driver's commands. The smart car will adopt active measures such as stopping the car in case the driver is unable to act properly, or applying passive protection to reduce possible harm in abrupt accidents, for example pop up airbags.

6.3   Context Modeling in Smart Car Space

A smart car aims at assisting its driver with easier driving, less workload and less chance of getting injured [10]. For this purpose, a smart car must be able to sense, analyze, predict, and react to the road environment, which is the key feature of smart cars: context-awareness.

Contexts consist of information collected when monitoring the roadway, the car and the driver. Nowadays, only a few types of contexts are utilized. Besides, most of the current smart cars lack complex reasoning. Therefore, we developed a context model based on the Hierarchical Context Model (details refer to Sect. 4.2) to implement a context-aware smart car space [7].

6.3.1   Context Atoms

Each sensor corresponds to a type of context atom. For each type of context atom, a descriptive name must be assigned to applications to use the contexts. We use ontology to define the name to guarantee the semantic understanding and sharing in smart cars. We use three ontologies as shown in Fig. 6.2.

(1) Ontology for environment contexts. The environmental contexts are related to physical environments. The ontology includes the description of weather, road surface conditions, traffic information, road signs, signal lamps and network status, etc.

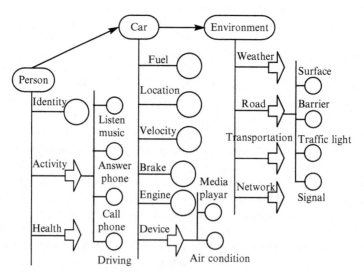

Fig. 6.2 Three ontologies for context atoms

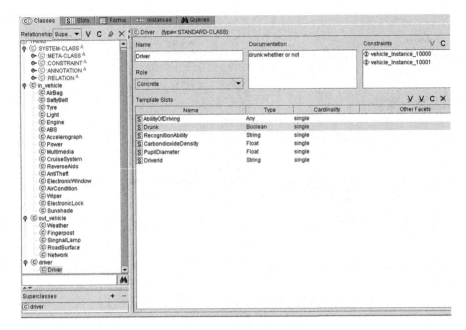

Fig. 6.3 Smart car ontologies implemented with protégé

(2) Ontology for car contexts. The car ontology includes three parts: the power system, the security system and the comfort system. The power system concerns the engine status, the accelerograph, the power (gasoline), etc. The security system includes factors related to the safety of the car and the driver, such as the status of the air bag, the safety belt, the ABS, the reversing-aids, the navigation system, the electronic lock, etc. The comfort system is about entertainment devices, the air conditioning and windows, etc.

(3) Ontology for driver contexts. The driver contexts are about the driver's physiological conditions, including heart beat, blood pressure, density of carbon dioxide, diameter of pupils, etc. The information is used to evaluate the healthy and mental status of the driver for determining whether he/she is able to continue driving.

We build the ontologies by protégé as shown in Fig. 6.3.

To use the context atoms, the subscription and publication mechanism are employed. Those applications interested in specific context atoms will be added to the subscriber list, along with information on how to publish context to them. Once a subscribed context changes, the new data will be delivered to the subscribing application.

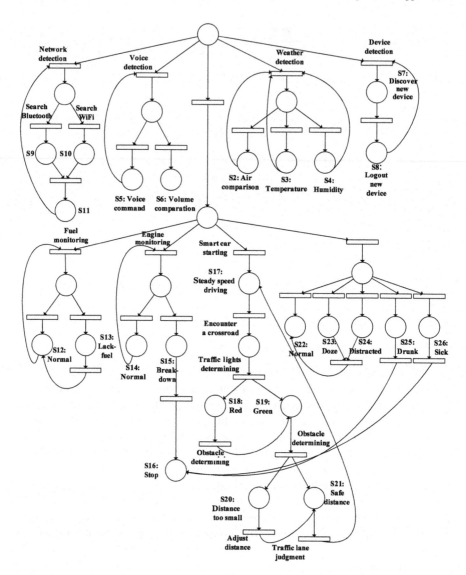

Fig. 6.4 The petri-net description of smart car space

6.3.2 Complex Context

Based on the definition in Sect. 4.2, we model a petri-net description of smart car space, as shown in Fig. 6.4. The model describes contexts from when a driver enters a smart car to when the driver arrives at the final destination. There are five typical scenarios in this petri-net description, which are:

(1) SCENARIO ONE: Smart Car Start

The initial context is a driver enters a car, and there are five parallel arcs starting from the initial context, which represent five parallel situations. Each of the five situations is independent and can occur without conflicts. Therefore, the token of the initial context is defined as 5.

The five situations are respectively: (1) weather detection: including temperature, air quality, humidity; (2) device discovery: detecting and discovering the new devices such as PDA, smart phone or Bluetooth MP4 Player in the smart car space; (3) network detection: detecting whether a wireless or Bluetooth network exists in the vicinity for data exchange and communication; (4) voice detection: determine whether the user is talking. If the voice is detected, judge whether the voice is a command or not. If the former, run a keyword-identification program and execute the corresponding command. Otherwise, adjust the background volume properly; (5) launch the car: begin a driving task. The conditions except (5) remain repeating, in order to detect the latest data change.

(2) SCENARIO TWO: Inside-Car Scenario When Driving

There are four parallel arcs, similar to scenario one, representing four parallel inside-car situations. The four situations are respectively: (1) Fuel monitoring: determining whether the remaining fuel is adequate for arriving at destination; There are two situations for fuel: when the amount of fuel is more than a certain value A, the status of fuel is "normal"; when the amount of fuel is less than a certain value B, the status of fuel is "lack-fuel". The status of fuel is in a critical state when the amount of fuel is between A and B, which is not described in Fig. 6.4 for simple and clear reasons. A smart car can only be in one of the two situations at any time, so we employ a conflict relationship to model the two states. (2) Engine monitoring: determining whether the engine is working properly. The status of engine is divided into "normal" and "breakdown". If a fault occurs, the car will stop for repair, so the status of a smart car become "stop". The relation between "normal" and "breakdown" is also a conflict. (3) Driver status monitoring: determining whether the driver is suitable for driving. The driver status includes "normal", "doze", "distracted", "drunk", and "sick". If the driver status is "doze" or "distracted", the system will make harsh noise to wake up driver. If the driver status is "drunk" or "sick", the system will make the car slowly stop for safe driving. (4) Driving behavior: this is concurrent with the above three kinds of monitoring and the detail will be described in scenario three.

(3) SCENARIO THREE: Outside-Car Scenario When Driving

This scenario focuses on judgement of the driving direction and speed adjustments according to traffic and road conditions.

When a driver encounters a crossroad or T-junction, the system determines whether traffic lights are red or green. If they are red, the system calculates the distance of the obstacle in front (including vehicles and boundary line of traffic lights). If distance is less than 1 m, the car will be slowed down and if the distance is less than 0.5 m, the car will be stopped to keep a safe distance from obstacles. If the traffic lights are green, the system determines whether the car turns or goes straight by traffic lane judgement. Afterwards, the status of the car becomes "steady speed".

(4) SCENARIO FOUR: Arriving At Destination

After arriving at the destination, the smart car turns off the engine and all electronic devices inside the car and checks the status of windows and doors for the sake of security.

6.4   Driver Behavior Modeling in Smart Car Space

In order to build a realistic smart car space, driver behavior models are required to be studied. At present, the research on driver behavior modeling is focused on three main directions: the driver performance and capacity, the longitudinal driver behavior models and driver skill models. The driver performance and capacity include mental [11] and physical research. The physical research includes fatigue [12], drugs [13,14], distraction (phone [15,16], entertainment [17]), etc. The mental research includes the effect on the changes in the driver environment. A longitudinal model describes vehicle acceleration behavior using throttle and brakes as inputting signals. The longitudinal driver behavior models include car-following, cutting-in, lane changing, etc. [18]. The driver's skills include steering, gears, brake, throttle, etc. There has been huge progress in all three directions in recent years [19].

One of the most important purposes of research into driver behavior is to resolve traffic safety problems. An independent research into driver behavior is meaningless. In this section, we introduce two aspect of driver behavior modeling for the smart car [20]:

(1) Comfortable and Safe Driver Behavior Model of Car-Following: Car-following is the most common driver behavior, and it's a typical research area of driver behavior. Car-following has become the basis of much research.
(2) Multi-Tasking Driver Behavior Model for the Smart Car: The driving task is an ever-changing set of basic tasks that are integrated and interleaved. Some of the tasks are not continuous but intermittent, arising from specific situations. Occasionally, two or more driving tasks have to be completed simultaneously within a very short period of time, which requires that driver tasks are handled in parallel.

6.4.1   Comfortable and Safe Driver Behavior Model
of Car-Following

Car-following is of interest because it is relatively simple compared to other driving tasks, and it has been successfully described by mathematical models. Also, it is an important facet of driving. Car-following research not only means an important contribution to the understanding of the traffic flow on roadways but also means a contribution to the avoidance of vehicle collisions on a motorway. Most of the early work on the car-following model [21], PD-controller car-following model [22], and visibility angle model [23, 24] show that drivers react immediately to the behavior of the vehicle in front of them so as to avoid imminent accidents. We will focus on the contribution to the passenger's comfort in the car in the following models.

6.4.1.1 A Car-Following Model Based on Space and Velocity

Most car-following models normally use several regimes to describe the follower's behavior. A common setup is to use three regimes: one for free driving, one for normal following, and one for emergency deceleration. Vehicles in the free regime are unconstrained and try to achieve their desired speed, whereas vehicles in the following regime adjust their speed with respect to the vehicle in front. Vehicles in the emergency deceleration regime decelerate to avoid a collision. The number of regimes used in the four programs varies between two and five. The following notation will be used throughout this section to describe the car-following models.

We consider a busy road with high flow rates, lane changing will be limited and a driver is forced to follow the car ahead. We assume that in this model a driver will follow the car in front of him with a time headway that allows him to stop just in time after seeing an emergency braking of the preceding car. We also assume that the braking decelerations of all cars are the same, and that the reaction times of the drivers are also the same. The two vehicles follow each other with speed V and space headway S. At time t the first vehicle brakes to stop, and at time $t + T$ the second vehicle starts to brake. When both vehicles stop, the space headway is exactly the length of the car L.

Car-following models describe the drivers longitudinal behavior in situations such as in Fig. 6.5. In these situations a driver is following another car and tries to maintain specific headway distance to the front car.

At the time of collision (assume that both the leading car and following car are in regular acceleration), to the following car:

$$2a(s + \Delta s) = \left(v'^2 - v^2\right) \tag{6.1}$$

To the preceding car:

$$2a\Delta s = \left(v_L'^2 - v_L^2\right) \tag{6.2}$$

As our purpose is to discuss the following car and the case with regard to the leading car is rather complicated, here we consider the worst condition while Δs is zero, and at the collision time the following car's velocity is also zero. Thus the car-following models can be simplified as

$$-2as = v^2 \tag{6.3}$$

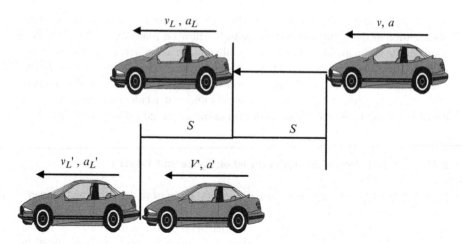

Fig. 6.5 Car-following model based on space and velocity

If we just consider the absolute value of acceleration, the above equation can be written as

$$2as = v^2 \qquad (6.4)$$

According to above formula, if the s and v are known, the acceleration a may be calculated immediately. If we know which acceleration value will make people feel comfortable or uncomfortable, we will limit the car's acceleration below this value. By applying this method the driver will avoid discomfort caused by rapid deceleration using the emergency brake. Fortunately, the researchers have found that the value of comfortable deceleration is $2\,\text{m/s}^2$, and this provides very useful information for our research model. To avoid a driver's discomfort caused by the rapid braking, when a car's deceleration exceeds the comfortable deceleration value, we will order the ECU (Electronic Control Unit) to slow down the car's speed.

6.4.1.2   Comfortable Car-Following Model Based on Acceleration

From Eq. (6.4), we know that there will be a definite acceleration to a different velocity v and distance s. To calculate the deceleration, we change the Eq. (6.5) into the following style:

$$a = v^2/(2s) \qquad (6.5)$$

where v represents the following car's velocity, s represents the distance between two cars, and a means the deceleration of the following car.

We represent the relationship s and v by using the diagram intuitively. Of the different accelerations a gives different curves shown in Fig. 6.6.

In order to avoid a following car collision with the preceding car, the distance between the two cars should be larger than zero, and the following car's velocity should be zero.

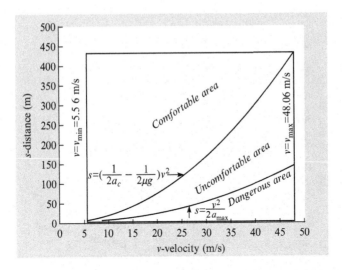

Fig. 6.6 The relationship between s and v to different a

$$a < v^2/(2s) \tag{6.6}$$

In Fig. 6.6, a_{max} is the maximum deceleration that the car can reach. It is definitely a special car and it can be calculated according to the following formula:

$$a_{max} = v_{max}/(2s_{min}) \tag{6.7}$$

where s_{min} is the minimum brake distance, and v_{max} is the maximum velocity the car can reach.

The curves $v = v_{max}$, $s = v^2/4$ and $s = v^2/(2a_{max})$ divide the first phrase into different areas. Of the different areas, there is a special physical conception parentally. Area A is surrounded by s-aix and $s = v^2/4$, its value is smaller than $a_c = 2m/s^2$, we call this area the comfortable area. Area B is surrounded by $v = v_{max}$, $s = v^2/4$ and $s = v^2/(2a_{max})$ and its value is larger than $a_c = 2m/s^2$ but smaller than a_{max}. We call this area the uncomfortable area. Area C is surrounded by $v = v_{max}$, $s = v^2/(2a_{max})$ and v-aix. Its value is larger than a_{max} and we call this area a very dangerous area.

6.4.1.3   Realization of Comfortable Driver Behavior Model

In real cases, the minimum brake distance is related to car's velocity; and the s_{min} is different according to the different velocity. It is also associated with the friction coefficient of the road surface and car. An experienced formula for this relationship is shown as follows:

$$s_{min} = v^2/(2\mu g) \tag{6.8}$$

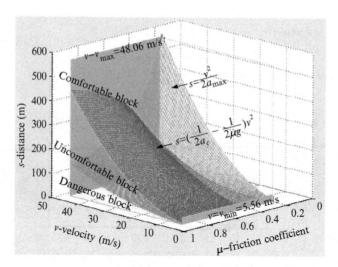

Fig. 6.7 The relationship among s, v, μ, and a

In real cases there are always some boundary conditions. For example, the maximum velocity is usually fixed to a certain car and when the velocity is below some value the passenger will not feel uncomfortable even in an emergency braking situation. We call it minimized comfortable velocity.

When considering the boundary conditions, we describe the relationships among a, s, v, μ in three dimensional diagrams. While different facets are circled by different spaces, the related space will represent a related physical conception like showed as Fig. 6.7.

6.4.2   Multitasking Driver Behavior Model for Smart Car Space

There are several theories as to how multiple tasks can be carried out at the same time, but they share the same basic idea that the cognitive system consists of several modules that can each operate asynchronously (independently) from each other [25]. An early version of this idea can be found in CPM-GOMS [26]. It is assumed that cognition, perception and motor actions can be done in parallel, although within each modality actions are serial. This idea is also the foundation of the EPIC [27] architecture, except that it assumes that cognitive actions can be done in parallel. Parallelization of behavior in these theories is a matter of optimizing the schedule of actions in all these modules. The APEX architecture [28] actually uses an algorithm to derive this optimal schedule. The EPIC modules are incorporated into the ACT-R architecture [25, 29]. However, ACT-R still assumes that central cognition is serial. Parallel behavior is often studied in dual-task experimental paradigms.

To figure out all these aspects, we employ the methods of the classification of the driver task, rank of risk level, and introduction of the subconscious to the ACT-R model, and improve ACT-R with a multi-production system, multi-monitor module and multi-motor module to realize the parallel process of multi-tasking driver behavior.

6.4.2.1 ACT-R Architecture and Driver Behavior Cognitive Model

ACT-R is a cognitive architecture, a theoretical model working mechanism of human cognition procedure. Researchers working on ACT-R strive to understand how people organize knowledge and produce intelligent behavior. From the exterior, ACT-R looks like a programming language; however, its constructions reflect assumptions about human cognition. These assumptions are based on numerous facts derived from psychology experiments. Researchers create models by writing them in ACT-R.

By writing the models using this type of programming language, they are adopting ACT-R's way of viewing human cognition. Researchers write their own assumptions in the model and test the model by comparing its results with the results of people actually performing the task.

One important feature of ACT-R that distinguishes it from other theories in the field is that it allows researchers to collect quantitative measures that can be directly compared with the quantitative measures obtained from human participants [30].

ACT-R has three main components: modules, buffers, and pattern matching. The architecture assumes a mixture of parallel and serial processing. Within each module there is a great deal of parallelism, and there are also two levels of serial bottlenecks in the system [30].

Of the special driving tasks, the ACT-R-based driver behavior model consists of at least three basic components, which are monitoring, decision-making and control (manipulation). The three components are integrated to run in ACT-R's serial cognitive processor as a tight loop of small cognitive (and related) operations. The entire model is implemented as an ACT-R production system including relevant procedural knowledge. And it takes advantage of the architecture's built-in features and human-like limitations that result in a more psychologically plausible model of driver behavior.

6.4.2.2 Multitasking Driver Cognitive Model

Three aspects related to the driver's parallel and multiprocessing behavior are discussed as follows, subconsciousness, parallel information processing, and parallel operations. The driver behavior classification and risk level criteria of behavior are also discussed.

Driver Subconscious/Unconscious Behavior

While driving, we often find that our reactions to certain situations are completely automatic when facing some urgent circumstance or in most normal situations. This is the subconscious/unconscious reaction. At least there are two benefits of these subconscious/unconscious processes: one is obviously the efficiency of handling the emergency. The other is that the automatic process will save a driver precious time and stamina in order to scan for potential dangers.

Therefore, the cognitive model should reflect all these aspects of human unconscious/subconscious behavior, i.e., some human behavior is a direct reaction directly to stimuli without going through the human brain. In order to map those subconscious/unconscious driver behavior, the MONITOR and MANUAL module are connected directly in the proposed ACT-R driver behavior model, and the model responds immediately to the external events without going through the production system of the ACT-R architecture.

Driver Behavior Parallel Processing

As we know, the human brain has many parts including the cerebral cortex, brain stem, and cerebellum. Injury in one part may only disrupt a particular step of an activity that occurs in that specific part. The research work eventually helps to show that the areas of the brain have specific functions though some functions are repeated. This is the idea known as parallel distributed processing [31].

Since a different cerebral area reacts to stimuli and events separately, and information is conducted in a parallel way, so the serial production system in ACT-R is not ideal. Therefore, we improve the ACT-R driver cognitive behavior model with multi-production threads. The related work shows that it fits the real cases well, and improves the model's efficiency for multi-tasking driver behavior processing.

Driver Behavior Classification

Michon discerns three driving task levels: strategic, tactical and operational. Driving typically involves all three types of processes working together to achieve a safe, stable navigation [32]. A driving task involves different parts (hand, foot and eye) of the body and physiological systems (neural, motor). Of all behavior, some has no relationships, while other behavior is inclusive or exclusive. Some operations can be executed in parallel, but other operations must follow different patterns. Some are urgent, but others are not.

Driver behaviors are classified here according to Michon's driving task level and related body parts [32, 33]. A strategic-level task is completed by the human brain and neural system, while a tactical-level task is completed by the monitor system, and hands or feet execute the related driving operations. The primary driver behavior and related body parts are listed in Table 6.1.

Table 6.1 Primary driver behavior and body parts

Body parts	Manual	Memo
Brain	Making decision	Making a sound decision
	Predicting	Predicting what will happen
	Identifying	Scanning for potential hazards
Eye	Looking ahead	Keeping eyes on ahead vehicle
	Looking Behind	Keeping eyes on rear mirror
	Looking dashboard	Checking information on dashboard
	Scanning	Keeping eyes moving to head road
	Looking to left side	Moving eyes anterior-left position
	Looking to right side	Moving eyes anterior-right position
	Checking vehicle's blind spots	Moving head and checking vehicle's blind spots
Left foot	Controlling clutch	Pushing, holding on and releasing clutch
	Pushing/releasing park	Pushing/releasing park peddle
Right foot	Braking	Pushing, holding on and releasing brake
	Accelerating	Pushing, holding on and releasing throttle
Both hand	Steering	Navigating
Left hand	Controlling light	Switching on/off light
Right hand	Shifting gear	Switching gear
	Controlling wash/swipe	Turning on/off wash/swipe

Driver Behavior Risk Level

There are different driver risk criteria. According to the Vehicle Incident Prevention Program High Risk Driving Criteria (Risk Management Division of Oregon Department of Administrative Services), marks are assigned based on the driving history and experience. The higher the final score, the greater the potential risk for a particular group of drivers and the agencies they represent. Reaction time to unexpected critical events is also being used to assess the differences in risk level. On-driving driver behavior risk level is applied here. It means that the risk level is defined according to the driver's driving situation and the environment. According to the estimated driver's hypovigilant state and the estimated level of traffic risk, the driver behavior risk level is categorized into five levels: high risk, moderate risk, low risk, contingency, and normal status.

(1) Normal status: There is no risk for a driving task of normal status. At this level, the driver handles a car freely. Even if there are cars in front of the driver's vehicle, it is at a safe distance and a driver can follow the car with the desired speed. There is no vehicle on either side of the driver's car, and there is no vehicle in the rear-mirror and the vehicle behind is far from being dangerous. Drivers can drive their car in a semi-conscious status, or the driver behavior is subconscious.

(2) Contingency: There are some unfavorable cases occurring for a driver. For example, the driver may find the distance between his car and the front one

is becoming smaller or the driver finds the vehicle following is approaching his car and wants to overtake. But at this level, the driver has enough time or skill to avoid any crash from happening, even if the driver needs not react to the appearing cases. For this level, drivers are in an awareness situation to avoid accidental fluctuation.

(3) Low-risk level: An example of this level is a pedestrian acrossing in a braking distance that is safe. Under this circumstance, drivers are in an awareness situation. Unsuitable or mistaken driver behavior can result in crashes. But in most cases experienced or even amateur drivers can handle the car skillfully and therefore the risk is still relatively low.

(4) Moderate risk level: An example of this level occurs when a pedestrian crosses in an unsafety braking. The sophisticated driver may avoid a crash, but an unsophisticated driver may not handle it skillfully enough to avoid it.

(5) An urgent or emergency situation often means a high-risk level. A sample scenario is when a pedestrian suddenly appears within a safe braking. High-risk level drivers are those who demonstrate a pattern of frequent crashes and severe violations. This requires more personalized attention. At this level, it is rather difficult to avoid accidents. While driving, the more dangerous the situation, the higher the priority. The urgent ones can interrupt those less urgent ones being processed. So the risk level is defined here as the priority of the driver's behavior. The primary principle is that an event with a high-risk level will interrupt an event with a lower level of risk. This way guarantees that urgent cases be handled first.

6.4.2.3 General Ideas of Multiprocessing and Parallel Driver Cognitive Behavior

For the purpose of model's efficiency and coincidence with the real world for driver multitasking, the parallel processing idea and subconscious behavior are conducted in the development of the ACT-R driver behavior model. Figure 6.8 show the general architecture of this improved model.

Parallel Production System Module

In order to process the multitask and solve the conflict of process priority at different risk levels, a register is applied to store the driver's behavior risk level for all the processing threads. When drivers perceive the irritation of a stimulus, an event, or a driving task that belongs to the subconscious/unconscious class, the model responds to it immediately and sends the related manipulation to the manual module directly for execution. Otherwise, the irritation reaches the model's production processing system through the visual buffer. The system compares the risk level with that of

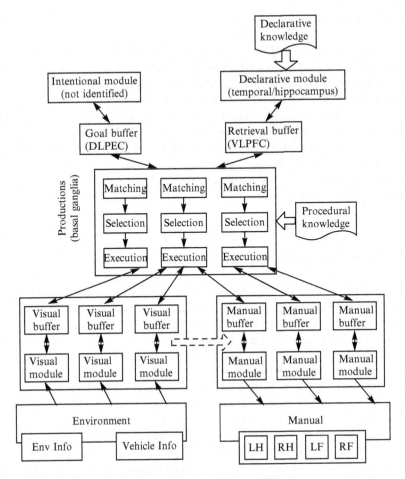

Fig. 6.8 Improved multitasking driver cognitive behavior model

the risk level register. If the risk level is less than, or equal to, the stored risk level and there is an empty production system thread, the irritation enters the SELECT and MATCH program. If there is no empty thread, it enters a queue to wait. If the risk level is higher than the risk level stored, and there is an empty production system thread, the irritation enters the SELECT and MATCH program. If there is no empty thread, the risk level in storage is replaced with the current irritation's risk level, and the irritation that is running in the production system is paused and enters the queue, i.e., the high risk level behavior enters the production system. After the completion of an irritation process, the risk level register is cleared and reset to zero. The thread of the production system is set to empty and waits for the next irritation. In the proposed model, three production system sub-modules are designed, and each of them has its own match, select and execute modules.

Parallel Driver Manipulation Module

Every production system or subconscious/unconscious reaction triggers the corresponding driver manipulation, which in turn results in a single driver operation. When manipulation is produced, the module probes whether or not there is exclusive manipulation in the other thread, and whether or not there are any joint operations in the declarative knowledge. If exclusive manipulations exist, the operation waits until the manipulation is finished. If there are joint operations, this operation and its joint operation are executed simultaneously on different manual modules. Otherwise, the operation is sent to the manual module to execute. In the proposed model, four parallel manual modules are concatenated to their own manual buffers. The related driver behavior correlates to left hand, right hand, left foot and right foot respectively.

Parallel Driver Monitor Module

Human beings with a complicated visual system have a wide field of vision, allowing them to resolve fine details, track a moving object, perceive depth, see colors and look in many directions. To see more, they have to move their entire head or even body. Yet the visual system in the brain is too slow to process that information if the images are slipping across the retina at more than a few degrees per second [34]. Thus, to be able to see while moving, the brain must compensate for the motion of the head by turning the eyes around. To get a clear view of the world, the brain must turn the eyes around so that the image of the object of our regard falls onto the fovea [35]. As we know, the movements of different body parts are controlled by striated muscles acting around joints. The movements of the eyes are with no exception. But they have special advantages that are not shared by skeletal muscles and joints, and so they are considerably different. When the muscles exert different tensions, a torque is exerted on the globe that causes it to turn. This is an almost pure rotation, with only about 1 mm of translation. Thus, the eye can be considered as undergoing rotations about a single joint in the eye's center [36]. Compared to the brain's slow processing, the eye's motion is rather rapid, and therefore we take the visual system as parallel input for the brain's different areas.

In contrast, the other parts of the body (such as ear and nose) may perceive and store the changing driving environment, such as the sound from somewhere close is a prediction that something may happen. There is also some subconscious/unconscious behavior in a driver's behavior we mentioned above. So drivers' monitoring the driving environment may not be in series, i.e., the model's monitor module should be in parallel processing mode. In our driver behavior model, three visual/monitor modules are designed to monitor the vehicle's running environment.

6.5 Prototype

We integrate services, devices, sensors, and networks to build a prototype of smart car space [6, 7]. An efficient network architecture is designed to communicate smoothly between mechanical equipment and smart devices, between smart devices, and between the in-car environment and the outer environment. A lightweight adaptive software infrastructure is developed to manage devices, support network communication and provide a runtime environment for the context model, driver behavior model and applications.

6.5.1 Network Infrastructure

The communications in the car space are shown in Fig. 6.9, consisting of four types of networks:

(1) Wireless sensor network: All mini-sensors in the car space, such as temperature sensor and acceleration sensor, are connected with the XMesh network, a

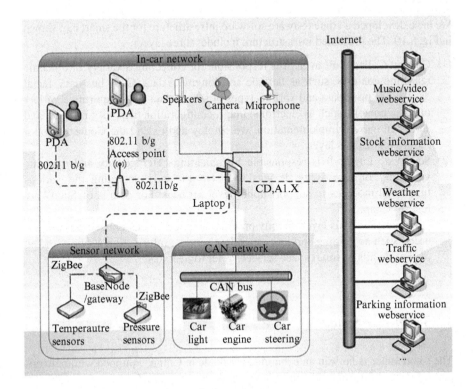

Fig. 6.9 Network architecture diagram in the smart car space

low-power wireless mesh networking stack by Crossbow Inc. XMesh supports the ZigBee sensor network standard. Our system employs Mica2/Dot Professional Mote Kit to build the sensor network.

(2) CAN (Controller Area Network) network: Many mechanical nodes in the car can use CAN bus to communicate, e.g., engine, steering system, window lock, car light. CAN [37] is a serial bus system for automotive applications to replace the complex wiring harness with a two-wire bus. CAN provides a multi-master hierarchy, broadcast communication, and sophisticated error detecting mechanisms.

(3) Wireless LAN network: Currently many high-end smart devices support 802.11a/b/g WLAN, like smart phones, PDAs, laptop computers. Our car space deploys a wireless access point to let it support 802.11b/g. We experiment with HP iPAQ Pocket PC H5500, which supports 802.11b.

(4) WAN network: We use the CDMA1X service of ChinaUnicom Corp. to keep the car accessing Internet at any time. In China, CDMA1.X provides coverages almost everywhere, and works relatively stably under the high-speed conditions.

6.5.2 Software Infrastructure

We have developed a context-aware software infrastructure for the smart car, shown in Fig. 6.10. The presented infrastructure includes three layers:

(1) Context Collection Layer: It is responsible for collecting a variety of dynamic real-time contexts, such as latitude and longitude data, CAN bus data, facial data, voice print data and various types of sensor data, and acquiring a variety of static context, such as electronic maps, configuration files, user profiles, and so on. In current implementation, we employ and extend the Context Toolkit [38] to realize this layer.

(2) ScudWare Layer: It is responsible for shielding heterogeneity and dynamic variability of underlying devices and sensors, and integrating the various functional modules to support upper-level services. For details of ScudWare refer to Chap. 5.

(3) Service Layer: This layer directly provides a variety of customized services for users, such as guiding service, car-follow service, information service, and so on. For details of smart space services refer to Sect. 6.4.

6.5.3 In-Car Space

The smart space is built in an economic car made in China, equipped with network and software infrastructures, smart devices, as shown in Fig. 6.11.

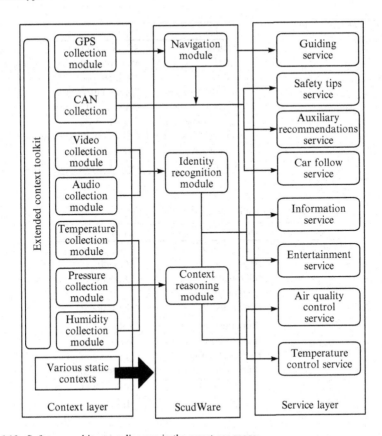

Fig. 6.10 Software architecture diagram in the smart car space

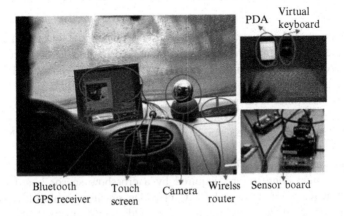

Fig. 6.11 A prototype of smart car space

Table 6.2 Device list in the smart car prototype

Device	Type
Notebook PC	SONY VAIO FJ
ECU	Motorola MPC555, Atmel AT89C51
PDA	400 MHz Intel, XScal-PXA255
Wireless router	D-Link DIR-300
CAN analyzer	CANalsyt-II
CAN connection	CANHub-S5
Virtual keyboard	I-tech virtual laser keyboard
Touch screen	FA801-NP/C/T, 8"
Camera	Logitech QuickCam Orbit

Table 6.3 Sensor list in the smart car prototype

	Sensor	Context
Environment	Thermometer	Temperature
	Hygrometer	Humidity
	Microphone	Loudness
	Ambient light sensor	Light
	IR sensors	Car following
Car	Hall-effect sensor	Velocity
	Hall-effect sensor	Wheel rotation
	Fuel level sensor	Fuel consumption
	Bluetooth GPS receiver	Car-location
	Accelerometer	Acceleration
Driver	Camera	Head, gaze, identity
	Microphone	Vocal command
	RFID	Identity
	Hand pressure sensor	Grip force
	Alcohol sensor	Alcohol density

The devices used in current implementation are listed in Table 6.2. A notebook PC runs the software platform and applications. A PDA conducts the cooperation with the software platform in the smart car. The virtual keyboard and the touch screen are used to provide the passengers with easier interaction. For communication, a wireless router is adopted to provide users with information services in the car. Three ECUs (Electronic Control Units) are built using an MPC555 processor. CAN hub is used to combine several communication nodes in a car. CAN analyzer is the necessary analysis tool for messaging.

Various sensors are deployed in our implementation, as listed in Table 6.3. The environment contexts are acquired by a crossbow sensor board, which is combined with a wireless module. It provides sensing capabilities including: ambient light, barometric pressure, magnetic field, photo-sensitive light, humidity, and temperature. Ultrasound sensors are used to estimate the distance between two adjacent cars.

The car contexts such as the information about fuel consumption, wheel rotation and velocity are obtained from the car CAN bus. A Bluetooth GPS receiver is used to determine the location of the car.

As for driver contexts, RFIDs are used to recognize the identity of the driver and passengers. A hand pressure sensor is used to determine the finger force on the steering wheel. An alcohol sensor is used to detect the alcohol level of the driver.

For simple sensors, all we need to do is to receive data from them. For complex sensors such as cameras and microphones, complicated processing is required after receiving the sensor data.

Cameras, commonly used for natural and unobtrusive detection, are installed to track the movement of eyes and the head of the driver. Real-time face detecting and eye tracking are achieved by fusion of ASM [39] and cascaded Adaboost [40]. Detection of blinking eye behavior is based on our previous work [41–43]. For image-based user recognition, we use the Fisherface algorithm [44] to compare the detected face with the registered users' face images.

A microphone is used to receive the vocal command from a driver. About 20 keywords, including "weather", "music on", "music off", "parking space", and so on, are defined for a driver to access services by voice rather than by hand. The SONAR [45], a speech processing and speaker recognition toolkit developed by our lab, is used to build the keyword recognition engine.

6.5.4 Services of Smart Car Space

One goal of smart car space is forming a spontaneous and customized service space in the car to provide appropriate services initiatively, reduce driver distraction, and build a safe, comfortable driving environment for users. Therefore, we designed and realized many services to set up the service space.

6.5.4.1 Smart Navigation

We have developed a GPS navigation system in smart car space to generate an optimum route for users by automatically perceiving or manually informing the users' destination. Our implementation uses the Microsoft SDK pronunciation engine to give tips on each action of the entire route by voice, such as changing direction and so on, greatly reducing the driving interference of users. Our smart navigation system consists of GPS receivers and electronic maps for navigation. The electronic map includes many data layers, such as facility layer, road layer, topology layer, and so on. The road layer, one layer in electronic maps, contains more than 20 parameters such as road direction, road height, maximum speed limit, maximum load-bearing, and so on. Therefore, electronic maps form a detailed database of the transportation network.

6.5.4.2   Safety Tips

Safe driving is an important and concerned issue in smart car space. To ensure driving safety, we collect current speed data from the CAN bus, and obtain the maximum speed limit from electronic map files. After comparison and analysis, we will remind the driver whether he is already speeding by voice.

In addition, we can obtain the road direction information (whether a one-way street) from the road layer of electronic maps, and the current direction of driving by VTG statements of the NEMA0183 protocol. Using the above two contexts, we can determine whether the driver retrogrades in a one-way road, and give the driver tips by voice.

6.5.4.3   Auxiliary Recommendations

As a smart space, smart car space automatically perceives the current state to give users some recommendations. We have designed a number of related services for users, including restaurant recommendations, gas station recommendations and parking recommendations.

If it is meal time, the system will combine latitude and longitude coordinates from GPS receivers with data of the user's tastes from the user database to recommend a nearby restaurant. If the system finds that the fuel will run out according to data from CAN bus, it automatically recommends a nearby gas station. If the system finds that navigation is about to be completed, it will automatically search and recommend a nearby parking place.

6.5.4.4   Entertainment Services

Our mobile music service realizes the migration of music playing. The whole system consists of a remote streaming media server, vehicle processing center, hand-held music players (such as PDA) and a detection device.

When the detection device detects the action of a user entering the car and the user's PDA is running remote music services, the vehicle processing center uses a custom protocol to obtain the current playback position from the PDA and connect the remote streaming media server to implement continuous and seamless migration of music playing. When the user leaves the car, the above procedure will be reversed to implement migration of music playing from the vehicle processing center to the PDA.

6.5.4.5   Information Services

In current implementation, we employ face and voice recognition to identify users. After that, we will provide several information services, such as news, stock prices, weather, and road conditions. These information services are implemented by a web service and provided by a remote web server. As the amount of provided information is tremendous, it must be screened based on current contexts and user profiles. For example, the system provides local weather information and news information which the user is interested in.

6.6 Conclusion

As a promising application domain of pervasive computing, a smart car space draws more and more attention. This chapter attempts to build a smart car space from the view of context-awareness. Our work mainly focuses on three aspects: (1) a general framework of the smart car space is set up; (2) a novel context model is proposed, which can represent complex driving contexts; (3) an improved driver behavior model for the smart car is proposed, including a comfortable car-following model and multi-tasking driver behavior model.

Moreover, we implement a prototype of smart car space, which includes network and software infrastructure. The current car space could be featured as: (1) Know where you are. (2) Know who you are. (3) Know when you talk. (4) Know where you should park. (5) Know your preference. (6) Support simple seamlessly mobile tasks. (7) Show what information you currently need.

Our future work includes applying more sophisticated sensing technologies to detect the physiological and psychological status of a driver to enhance the smart car space prototype. Knowledge-based inference approaches will be developed and asserted into the risk assessment for more reliable decision-making. More considerations and efforts will be made to predict driver intention predictions.

References

1. Jochemi T, Pomerleau D, Kkmar B, Armstrong J (1995) PANS: a portable navigation platform. In: IEEE symposium on intelligent vehicle, Detroit
2. Conti JP (2006) Smart cars. Commun Eng 3(6):25–29
3. Oliver N, Pentland AP (2000) Driver behavior recognition and prediction in a Smart Car. In: Verly JG (ed) Enhanced and synthetic vision 2000, Orlando, USA. SPIE proceedings series, vol. 4023. SPIE, Bellingham, pp 280–290
4. Siewiorek D, Smailagic A, Hornyak M (2002) Multimodal contextual car-driver interface. In: Martin DC (ed) 4th IEEE international conference on multimodal interfaces (ICMI'02), Washington, DC, IEEE Computer Society Press, pp 367–373
5. Wang FY, Zeng D, Yang LQ (2006) Smart cars on smart roads: an IEEE intelligent transportation systems society update. IEEE Pervasive Comput 5(4):68–69
6. Pan G, Wu ZH, Sun J (2007) Towards a smart space inside car. In: The 9th international conference on ubiquitous computing (Ubicomp'07), LBR, Innsbruck, Austria, 16–19 Sept 2007

7. Sun J, Wu ZH, Pan G (2009) Context-aware smart car: from model to prototype. J Zhejiang Univ (Scie A) 10(7):1049–1059
8. Tang SM, Wang FY, Miao QH (2006) ITSC 05: current issues and research trends. IEEE Intell Syst 21(2):96–102
9. Rau PS (1998) A heavy vehicle drowsy driver detection and warning system: scientific issues and technical challenges. In: Proceeding of 16th international technical conference on the enhanced safety of vehicles (ESV98), Ontario, Canada
10. Moite S (1992) How smart can a car be?. In: Proceedings of the intelligent vehicles'92 symposium. IEEE Press, Los Alamitos, pp 277–279
11. Waard DD (1996) The measurement of drivers' mental workload. PhD thesis, Traffic Research Centre, University of Groningen, Haren, The Netherlands
12. Haworth NL, Triggs TJ, GreyDriver EM (1988) Driver fatigue: concepts, measurement and crash countermeasures. Technical report, Federal Office of Road Safety Contract Report 72 by Human Factors Group, Department of Psychology, Monash University, Melbourne
13. Veeraraghavan H, Papanikolopoulos NP (2001) Detecting driver fatigue through the use of advanced face monitoring techniques, artificial intelligence, robotics, and vision laboratory. Department of Computer Science and Engineering, University of Minnesota, Twin Cities. http://www.its.umn.edu/Publications/ResearchReports/reportdetail.html?id=517. Retrieved 25 Apr 2013
14. Bevan J (1998) Drugs and driving: a discussion paper. AA Group Public Policy, Basingstoke
15. Alm H, Nilsson L (1995) The effects of a mobile telephone task on driver behavior in a car following situation. Accid Anal Prev 27(5):707–715
16. McKnight AJ, McKnight AS (1993) The effect of cellular phone use upon driver attention. Accid Anal Prev 25(3):259–265
17. Burns P (2003) Strategies for reducing driver distraction from in-vehicle telematics devices: a discussion document. Transport Canada, Road Safety and Motor Vehicle Regulation Directorate
18. Fang XP (2001) Driver behavior models for traffic simulation. Master's thesis, Iowa State University. Transport Canada, Road Safety and Motor Vehicle Regulation Directorate
19. Yoshiyuki U (2004) Driver behavior and active safety (Overview). RD Rev Toyota CRDL 39(2):1–8
20. Wu ZH, Liu YF, Pan G (2009) A smart car control model for brake comfort based on car following. IEEE Trans Intell Transp Syst (TITS) 10(1):42–46
21. Bengtsson J (2001) Adaptive cruise control and driver modeling. Lund University, Sweden
22. Fang XP, Phaml HA, Kobayashi M (2001) PD controller for car-following models based on real data. In: 1st human-centered transportation simulation conference, Iowa City, Iowa
23. Pipes LA, Wojcik CK (1968) A contribution to theory of traffic flow. In: Analysis and control of traffic flow symposium, Detroit, USA, Society of Automotive Engineers, pp 53–60
24. Reijmers IJJ (2003) Traffic guidance systems. Society of Automotive Engineers, Et4-024
25. Taatgen N (2005) Modeling parallelization and flexibility improvements in skill acquisition: from dual tasks to complex dynamic skills. Cogn Sci 29(3):421–455
26. Gray WD, John BE, Atwood ME (1993) Project Ernestine: Validating a GOMS analysis for predicting and explaining real-world performance. Hum Comput Interact 8(3):237–309
27. Meyer DE, Kieras DE (1997) A computational theory of executive cognitive processes and multiple-task performance. Part 1. Basic mechanisms. Psychol Rev 104:2–65
28. Matessa M, Remington R, Vera A (2003) How apex automates CPMGOMS. In: 5th international conference on cognitive modeling, Bamberg, Germany, pp 93–98
29. Byrne MD, Anderson JR (2001) Serial modules in parallel: the psychological refractory period and perfect time-sharing. Psychol Rev 108(4):847–869
30. Anderson JR, Bothell D, Byrne MD (2004) An integrated theory of the mind. Psychol Rev 111(4):1036–1060
31. Kandel ER (2001) The molecular biology of memory storage: a dialogue between genes and synapses. Science 294(5544):1030–1038

32. Michon JA (1985) A critical view of driver behavior models: what do we know, what should we do?. In: Evans LA, Schwing RC (eds) Human behaviour and traffic safety. Plenum Press, New York, pp 485–520

33. Salvucci DD (2006) Modeling driver behavior in a cognitive architecture. Hum Factors 48:362–380

34. Westheimer G (1954) Eye movement responses to horizontally moving visual stimuli. Arch Ophthalmol 52:932

35. Grzywacz NM, Watamaniuk SN, McKee SP (1995) Temporal coherence theory for the detection and measurement of visual motion. Vision Res 35(22):3183–3203

36. Carpenter RHS (1988) Movements of the eyes, 2nd Rev. Pion Ltd., London

37. CAN in Automation. http://www.can-cia.org. Retrieved 25 Apr 2013

38. Salber D, Dey AK, Abowd GD (1999) The context toolkit: aiding the development of context-enabled applications. In: Williams MG, Altom MW (eds) Proceedings of the SIGCHI conference on human factors in computing systems (CHI'99), Pittsburgh, PA, ACM, pp 434–441

39. Cootes TF, Edwards GJ, Taylor CJ (2001) Active appearance models. IEEE Trans Med Imaging 23(6):681–685

40. Viaola P, Jones MJ (2004) Robust real-time face detection. Int J Comput Vis 57(2):137–154

41. Pan G, Sun L, Wu ZH, Lao SH (2007) Eyeblink-based anti-spoofing in face recognition from a generic webcamera. In: 11th IEEE international conference on computer vision (ICCV'07), Rio de Janeiro, Brazil, pp 1–8

42. Pan G, Wu ZH, Sun L (2008) Liveness detection for face recognition. In: Delac K, Grgic M, Bartlett MS (eds) Recent Adv Face Recognit. InTech, pp 109–124

43. Sun L, Pan G, Wu ZH, Lao SH (2007) Blinking-based live face detection using conditional random fields. In: The 2nd international conference on biometrics (ICB'07), Seoul, Korea, 27–29 Aug 2007

44. Belhumeur PN, Hespanha JP, Kriegman DJ (1997) Eigenfaces vs. Fisherfaces: recognition using class specific linear projection, IEEE Trans Pattern Anal Mach Intell 19(7):711–720

45. Liu YY (2007) Sonar 2.0: the speaker recognition software platform. Master's thesis, Zhejiang University, China (in Chinese)

Index

Z. Wu and G. Pan, *SmartShadow: Models and Methods for Pervasive Computing*, Advanced Topics in Science and Technology in China, DOI 10.1007/978-3-642-36382-5, © Zhejiang University Press, Hangzhou and Springer-Verlag Berlin Heidelberg 2013

Printed in the United States
By Bookmasters